HOW TO CREATE
YOUR OWN
JEWELRY LINE

✦

EMILIE SHAPIRO

LARK
New York

An Imprint of Sterling Publishing
1166 Avenue of the Americas
New York, NY 10036

ISBN 978-1-4547-0933-6

Distributed in Canada by Sterling Publishing
c/o Canadian Manda Group, 664 Annette Street
Toronto, Ontario, Canada M6S 2C8
Distributed in the United Kingdom by GMC Distribution Services
Castle Place, 166 High Street, Lewes, East Sussex, England BN7 1XU
Distributed in Australia by Capricorn Link (Australia) Pty. Ltd.
P.O. Box 704, Windsor, NSW 2756, Australia

For information about custom editions, special sales, and premium and corporate purchases, please
contact Sterling Special Sales at 800-805-5489 or specialsales@sterlingpublishing.com.

Manufactured in China

2 4 6 8 10 9 7 5 3 1

larkcrafts.com

HOW TO CREATE
YOUR OWN
JEWELRY LINE

✦

Contents

✦

Introduction

✦

Over the years, thousands of students have attended classes I've taught, hoping to learn jewelry production, mostly so they can start their own jewelry line. After some research, I was surprised to find that there was a scarcity of resources on this topic. Students could pick up only bits and pieces of information here and there about how to market their jewelry, but most people just didn't know where to start or how to make a big push.

I have found the majority of people in the jewelry industry—and most industries—to be very secretive when it comes to sharing trade insights, contacts, best practices, and trials and errors of their own path. After getting loads of questions about this from my students, I decided to teach a lecture-style class about jewelry production. The response was overwhelming.

Through years of experience holding many different jobs in diverse facets of the jewelry industry, I have learned from my mistakes and accomplishments and have applied all those lessons to building my own company. In writing this book, my goal is to share the insights I have gained with aspiring designers to help them become successful jewelry designers and business owners. I am extremely proud to be writing this book, and to make this information available to a large audience.

I have always had a knack for design and business, but it took me many years to develop the skills and the patience of a craftsperson. From my earliest days, I was interested in designing and creating things. My father worked in sales at a fabric mill in New York City's garment district, so fabric samples in all sorts of patterns were always available in my playroom. I have fond memories of wandering the sample floor high above Eighth Avenue and learning about color and texture. When I was five, I loved designing and making clothes for my dolls. Using my (not-so) safety scissors, I would cut up my fabric to make outfits for my dolls.

I made my first piece of jewelry when I was thirteen and haven't stopped since then. After my grandmother passed away, I found a bag of her costume jewelry. I was always fascinated by how things were made, so I started taking apart my grandmother's necklaces, bracelets, and brooches and putting them back together in a new way. Focusing on design, rather than construction, I haphazardly assembled my own pieces, but they always fell apart. When I was in high school, I started selling my jewelry to friends, family, and the people who would watch me make it while I was working at a local beach club. My designs were strong, but the craftsmanship was weak.

Running a jewelry production business is different from being an artist. An artist can focus solely on design and aesthetics. A jewelry entrepreneur must be concerned about the customer's satisfaction after the purchase. You're looking to create a piece that will be cherished and passed down from generation to generation.

I didn't learn this until many years later, but it takes time to hone your craft. It calls for a lifetime of research, discipline, trial and error, and learning from your mistakes. Certain things come naturally to each of us, and certain things have to be learned. Design and business were always strong suits for me. I knew two things: I wanted to be my own boss and I wanted to make original pieces that would be treasured for years to come.

Since I was interested in accessories, I enrolled in Syracuse University to pursue a career in fashion design. In the first semester of my freshman year, I almost failed my Sewing 101 class because I didn't follow the patterns and didn't care what my seams looked like. Again, my stuff looked cool but didn't last. At this point, I was selling my jewelry designs out of my dorm room, when a professor suggested I take a metalsmithing class. To me, metalsmithing sounded like a genre of music, one that scared the classic rock lover in me. I can still remember the smell of the studio on my first day of class. I felt like I was home and was connected with something, but didn't know why. With every skill and technique I learned, I grew more and more excited. My mind always knew where I wanted to go and what I wanted to make, but I didn't yet have the skill set to pull it off.

I loved working with metal because you could see the effort you put into it in the final product; there was no hiding in metal. In true Emilie fashion, I never cared if my solder seams were perfect or my edges were filed nicely. In fact, I don't remember ever polishing my work while in school. I was so focused on starting a business that I would sell all my projects from class. I never understood why my professors encouraged me to perfect my craft first and then start a business.

When I was nineteen, I boarded a plane to Florence, Italy, with an overpacked suitcase filled with sandals, sundresses, and my jeweler's saw. I had nothing more than an address on a sticky note to tell me where to go when the plane landed. I had been accepted into an independent study program at Alchimia, a well-known contemporary jewelry school just outside of Florence, in an artists' and young professionals' neighborhood called San Frediano. I remember getting out of the taxicab on via de Burchiello and ringing the bell of a three-story row house, hoping I was in the right place. I met my summer roommates, and, to my surprise, they were all jewelry students. In fact, almost everyone who lived in my building was a jeweller. At Syracuse University, there were just five people in my major. The year I graduated, there was only one other girl who had majored in metalsmithing. I would tell fellow students that I was a metalsmithing major, and they just assumed I made knives and brass knuckles.

On my first day of class at Alchimia, we didn't even touch a piece of metal. In fact, I don't think I worked with metal the entire time I was there. We talked about the idea of jewelry and the concepts behind our work. We designed pieces to entice our senses, not to look pretty. We talked about materials, and what would happen if you mixed sea salt with resin (it never cured, and I made a huge mess). What I learned while I was studying in Florence was how far I could push myself—not just physically, but mentally, too. When you create something and put something into the world, you're infusing it with meaning. I learned to think beyond the traditional techniques, to experiment with materials. I learned to problem solve—to come up with a design and figure out how to make it. And to make it well. I made more pieces that summer than I had in the previous two years of college.

Looking back, that summer in Italy was a turning point in my life and my career. Alchimia had taught me to take pride in good craftsmanship and understand that I had a lot more to learn before I could sell my work. After I graduated from college, I took an internship on the jeweler's bench with Pamela Love Jewelry, a young designer who already had a cult following for her edgy jewelry inspired by botany, astrology, and astronomy. During my time there as a bench jeweler, I did the same thing every day—clean castings, cut, grind, sand, polish, repeat. As monotonous as it sounds, I really honed my skills there. Doing the same thing every day, you build muscle memory and strength, and train your hands to become fine-tuned instruments. I remember thinking, for the first time, that my hands knew what to do without my even thinking about it. I was amazed by how much work we were producing every day.

Later, I became the production manager of the rapidly growing company. Truth be told, I was in way over my head, but I learned a great deal about producing a jewelry line in-house in this position. Pamela's dedication to sustainability and keeping as much of the production in our studio as possible, planted a very large seed in my mind. While I was there, I was in charge of taking the prototypes to production and overseeing production from start to finish for wholesale and retail orders. We grew from having one in-house bench jeweler, to having a team of five just in the year I was there. I learned that what makes a production line successful is a good jewelry model of your first piece with clear production systems in place.

I left Pamela Love because I wanted to pursue another passion of mine—teaching. I was always drawn to education; it's in my blood. My mom is a schoolteacher, and my sisters had each taught in their respective fields—culinary arts and law. While I was in college, I was a teacher's assistant in a few classes and I loved sparking a passion in students that left them wanting to learn more. I taught my first workshop at Liloveve Jewelry Studio, a small boutique studio in Brooklyn, New York. I learned how to teach there, how much I loved it, and that the teacher is also a student. I remember a moment while teaching an Introduction to Silversmithing class. I was helping a student solder a ring and all of a sudden it just clicked. By explaining how to solder many different ways, I felt that I finally knew how to control the metal, the heat, and the solder, instead of being a bystander in a process while following steps that just somehow worked.

Eventually, I became the program director of Liloveve Jewelry Studio, creating exciting classes and workshops and developing curriculums for people who were passionate about jewelry. I found that most of our students—people already in the industry or looking for a creative outlet—wanted to learn another skill, and planned to create their own jewelry line. We prided ourselves on being a bridge between the jewelry industry and the ancient techniques and craftsmanship. I have taught thousands of students at the 92nd Street Y, the Brooklyn Museum, the Newark Museum, the Brooklyn Brainery, and the Art League of Long Island, and I still teach today.

When I was planning to launch my own jewelry line, I wanted to structure it as a handmade line focusing on wholesale distribution, similar to how we operated at Pamela Love. My style came from the mix of my education and experience, focusing on good craftsmanship and experimentation with materials. I used lost-wax casting for its accessibility, versatility, and the possibilities it offered to use recycled metals. I aimed to strike a balance between the art jewelry world and the production world.

I'm inspired by the beauty in imperfection—whether those imperfections come from the natural gemstone, the texture, or the technique. I hope the wearers of my jewelry see a reflection of themselves in my work, celebrating both imperfections and natural beauty.

When I started my line, I began approaching local stores to sell my work. After picking up a few accounts, I had a little momentum and reached out to stores across the United States after doing lots of research on stores I genuinely thought would be a good fit. I was working incredibly hard, reaching out to retailers to carry my line and trying out craft fair after craft fair, searching for my market. I was having a hard time selling pieces that cost $200 across the row from people whose jewelry was selling for $20 apiece. At this time, my work was something of a hodgepodge of techniques I had learned in school and through experimentation with materials. I didn't have a cohesive brand, just an array of pieces.

Another jeweler recommended that I reach out to Fab.com, a company at the time known for flash sales and highlighting indie designers. I arranged for a three-day sale, and although I felt I was in way over my head, not knowing how much work to make or what to expect, I had a deadline. This deadline gave me the motivation I needed to get my line in order and actually get it done. My sale was highly successful and gave my brand the push it needed. I got a lot of recognition from wholesale and retail accounts, but most of all I got the largest check I had ever seen for selling my jewelry.

I used the money to invest in my first trade show. I had heard of trade shows, but I had never attended one, much less exhibited at one. I went into my first trade show blind and put my resources and energy in the wrong place. I totally tanked. I was lucky enough to get one big order from a gallery owner who still buys my work today, but I didn't break even. My first trade show—every show, really—was a huge learning experience. I learned about display and merchandising, line sheets and marketing, how to expand my line to sell better, and much more. At my second show, I did markedly better, but it was still a learning experience. I significantly changed the way I displayed and merchandised my work. As a result, I actually had people looking at my line and ordering my work at the show.

Many shows and many learning experiences later, my work is sold internationally at specialty boutiques, museum shops, galleries, and department stores. I grew from creating my work in a dilapidated, shared, windowless Brooklyn studio with fake three-quarter walls, to having my own studio and showroom with a small, in-house team of bench jewelers and sales and marketing assistants. I feel grateful every day that I own my business and have generated jobs for creative people, but, most of all, that I get to share my wearable artwork with people around the world. I am passionate about educating aspiring designers on all aspects of running a handmade jewelry line.

I hope you use this book as a tool in building your own business and sharing your work with others. I've included everything I know, as well as a section filled with insider tips, a glossary of terms, and a detailed vendor list to get you started. I am a big believer in sharing our knowledge with others, in hopes they, too, will be successful. By educating each other and our consumers, we are building a collective consciousness, which will help create support for and grow the market for handmade jewelry. The more we support each other, the more people will support the handmade movement.

CHAPTER 1

Business Essentials

✦

Abusiness without a goal is just a hobby. Owning a jewelry business is much more than making pretty things. The biggest difference between running a business and engaging in a hobby is the goal: you're running a business to make money. More and more people are pursuing the life of entrepreneurship, becoming their own boss. Being a designer and a creator is an amazing gift, but when you decide to become a business owner, your main goal is to make money.

Running a business is not for everyone. It requires a lot of persistence and ambition. As a craft business owner, you are focusing on efficiency over creativity. Making jewelry is just one small part of running a jewelry business.

Craft businesses range from individuals who earn extra cash from their part-time business to designers who own and manage substantial companies with skilled employees.

HOW TO FORM YOUR BUSINESS

There are many different types of businesses, and figuring out which is best for you can seem overwhelming. Here is a breakdown of the most common types of businesses you can form, with a list of the advantages and disadvantages of each one. If you are not sure which is best for you, ask a professional—an accountant, an attorney, or a business consultant—to help point you in the right direction. Oftentimes, local governments offer free advice and resources, so take advantage of that as well.

The most basic forms of business are sole proprietorships, if you are one person who owns the business, and partnerships, if there is more than one business owner. They are easy to create and maintain, and don't require any start-up fees. However, when you establish one of these business entities you have unlimited liability, meaning you are personally liable for all business debts and other liabilities. To incorporate your business as a limited liability company (LLC) or corporation, you must pay fees and draft formation documents that must be filed with the appropriate agencies in your state, but these types of business entities shield you from unlimited liability. That means your personal assets are protected and the business is a completely separate entity. Incorporating as an LLC or a corporation helps protect your personal assets, while sole proprietorships and partnerships leave you open to unlimited liability.

Sole Proprietorships

ADVANTAGES

Easy to create and maintain; no
    start-up fees.
You own the business and all the assets.

You can deduct a net business loss from
    your personal income tax.

DISADVANTAGES

You are personally liable for any debt or
    other business liabilities.
You must pay personal income taxes on
    all net profits from the business.

Partnerships

ADVANTAGES

Easy to create and maintain; no
    start-up fees.
Owners can deduct their share of any
    business loss on their personal income
    tax returns.

DISADVANTAGES

Owners are personally liable for debts
    and other liabilities of the business.

Limited Liability Companies

ADVANTAGES

Owners of the business have limited
    liability when it comes to business
    debts and other liabilities.
Owners' losses are limited to their
    investment in the company.
Owners choose how the business will be
    taxed, either as a partnership or as a
    corporation.

DISADVANTAGES

More expensive to establish than a sole proprietorship or a partnership. Owners may have to pay annual registration fees to the government.

Revenue generated by the LLC is taxable, as is money paid to the owners as salary.

Corporations

ADVANTAGES

Owners of the business have limited liability when it comes to business debts and other liabilities.

Your losses are limited to your investment in the company.

DISADVANTAGES

More expensive to establish than a sole proprietorship or a partnership. The corporation may have to pay annual registration fees to the government.

A more complex corporate structure; generally suggested for larger companies with multiple employees.

Complicated paperwork is required to form the business and must be filed with the secretary of state in the state where the business is incorporated.

The corporation pays its own taxes as a separate tax entity.

Filing a DBA

A DBA, or "doing business as," allows a company to conduct day-to-day business under another name. This is usually filed in the county where the business is established, so check with your local government about what you need to do to set up a DBA. For example, my limited liability company, Emilie Shapiro Studio, LLC, does business as Emilie Shapiro Contemporary Metals.

TAXES AND LICENSES

Taxpayer Identification Number

A taxpayer identification number (TIN) is a generic term used by the Internal Revenue Service (IRS) for a number assigned to your business to be used for tax purposes on all documents and forms.

Social Security Number

If you are a sole proprietor or you have an LLC with no employees, you can use your Social Security number (SSN) for tax purposes, since the business files and pays taxes through the owner's personal tax return.

Employer Identification Number

If you operate as a corporation or a partnership, you are required to get an employer identification number, or an EIN. You are also required to get an EIN if your business employs workers and withholds taxes from their wages and salaries. Each EIN is unique, just as your Social Security number is. The IRS requires your business to put the EIN on all your tax documents as a form of identification. To get an EIN, apply for one by visiting the IRS website or calling the IRS.

Seller's Permit and Resale Certificate
Depending on what state you live in and your local jurisdiction, you will be required to register for a seller's permit and/or a resale certificate. In certain areas they are one and the same. A seller's permit allows a government entity to recognize a business as a collector of sales tax. Some states call this a sales tax permit. If you are selling your jewelry to retail customers, you are required to collect sales tax and then report total sales to the government annually if you owe under a few thousand dollars in sales tax, and quarterly if you owe more. Check with your local government for the appropriate way to file your sales tax for your business.

If you are selling your work online, sales tax is collected only if the purchaser lives in your tax jurisdiction. If you are shipping your work out of state, there is no sales tax collected. For example, if your office is in New York and someone from Ohio purchases a necklace from you online, she does not owe any sales tax. If someone who lives in New York purchases your work, however, he is charged sales tax.

If you are selling your jewelry at a craft market, you are required to collect the sales tax for the jurisdiction you are in. If you are selling at a market out of state, you must collect, report, and pay the sales tax for that state. Contact the state government to receive the appropriate paperwork and register to collect sales tax there.

A resale certificate specifies that a business can sell supplies tax-free if they are used to manufacture a product and be resold down the line, or can purchase wholesale items to resell. Sales tax is collected down the road when the item is sold to the final customer. The seller of the original items is required to get a copy of the resale certificate to keep on file for tax purposes. For example, if you are purchasing jewelry-making supplies, you will need to give a copy of your resale certificate to the supplier to ensure that your purchase is tax-free. If you are selling your products wholesale, you need a copy of the buyer's resale certificate to have on file to prove that the buyer can make the purchase tax-free and will charge tax when the product is sold to the final customer.

Collecting and Paying Taxes

PAYING SALES TAX

If you are selling your products to retail channels in person, at craft markets, or online, you will collect sales tax at the time the customer purchases the item from you. The sales tax you collect is then paid to the state periodically, depending on the volume of sales you make and the state where your business is established. Check your state government's website for sales and use tax return forms and instructions on when and how often to file your sales tax.

Generally, the more revenue you bring in, the more often you will file to pay your sales tax throughout the year. You may need to file annually, quarterly, or monthly, so check with your local jurisdiction for the appropriate forms to file your sales tax.

ESTIMATED TAX PAYMENTS

Unless you expect to owe under $1,000 in taxes for the entire year, as a small business owner you need to make estimated tax payments quarterly throughout the year to cover your federal tax liability. Although this sounds like a lot, it's much better to pay your taxes four times a year than to have one large sum due all at once. The four estimated tax payments are due on April 15, June 15, September 15, and January 15. Use Form 1040-ES if you are mailing your payments to the IRS. You can also pay electronically through the IRS website by enrolling in the Electronic Federal Tax Payment System.

Employees or Independent Contractors

If you hire someone to work for you, it's important to establish right away if she is an employee or an independent contractor. Independent contractors generally supply their own equipment and/or materials and have control over their flexible schedule. An employee generally relies on the business for a set schedule with steady income and is eligible for certain benefits. Your tax liability and what you report is different for each one. For independent contractors, you don't pay or withhold employment tax, as you would for an employee. At the end of the year, you will report how much you paid any independent contractor using a 1099-MISC form. For employees, you must pay a share of their Social Security and Medicare taxes and withhold their share of those taxes from their wages.

When hiring a new employee, there is information that you need to collect for your records and forms you need to complete. Have the prospective employee fill out Form I-9, Employee Eligibility Verification, to verify they are able to work in the

United States. Collect your new employee's full legal name and Social Security number for Form W-2. You should have a Form W-4, Employee's Withholding Allowance Certificate, to know how much income tax to withhold from the employee's wages. This should be completed before the employee begins working for you.

Bank Accounts

When you're operating as a business, you need to establish a bank account exclusively for business income and expenses. This is separate from your personal account. You can visit the bank of your choice in person or go online to open your bank account. Depending on what type of business you formed, you will need your SSN or EIN, personal photo identification, your business license showing the name(s) of the owner(s), and a copy of your business name filing document or business organizing document, which was filed with your state to form your business.

BUSINESS VERSUS PERSONAL EXPENSES

It is very important to keep your business and your personal expenses separate. Business expenses are deductible for federal tax purposes. Personal expenses are not deductible. For federal tax purposes, you are allowed to deduct ordinary and necessary expenses while running your business. To the IRS, **ordinary expenses** are those "common and accepted in your trade, business, and profession" and **necessary expenses** are "appropriate and helpful to your business. An expense doesn't have to be required to be helpful."

TYPICAL EXPENSES INCLUDE:

Travel expenses: food and lodging, entertainment, and gifts, when work requires you to be away from home

Local transportation: travel between workplaces, but not commuting from work to home

Professional or business organizations, subscriptions to trade publications, and the like

Work clothes or uniforms required for work, but not suitable to wear anywhere else

Business-related legal fees

Home office expenses, provided the space is used regularly for work

Accepting Credit Cards

Accepting credit cards is vital in today's business world, and there are many easy and inexpensive options to do so. Paying monthly rent for a credit card terminal is becoming outdated. Instead, mobile point-of-sale applications are gaining popularity.

Check with your bank to see if the bank has a mobile point-of-sale option. Many large banks provide these options at competitive rates. Companies like Square and PayPal offer a free credit card reader that attaches to your smartphone or other mobile device, and free use of their application makes it simple and seamless to accept credit cards with standard rates. You can swipe a customer's credit card if you are processing the order in person, or key in the credit card numbers for a slightly higher fee.

Credit card processing companies make their money by charging a small fee for every transaction. It is standard for a processing company to collect 2.5–3.5 percent for each credit card charge. Credit card processing companies try to give you the best competitive rate so you will use their service. However, with companies like Square and PayPal, which have established fixed low rates with no hidden fees, it is hard to find another company that can beat those rates.

Insurance

Insurance coverage is available for every imaginable risk your business may encounter. Cost and coverage vary widely, so talk with an insurance broker about what you want your insurance to cover. Insurance coverage is a form of risk management that is essential for every kind of business. There are specific types of insurance geared toward owning a jewelry business and manufacturing company that you should also consider.

General liability insurance is the most basic kind of insurance. This covers your legal responsibilities for accidents and other injuries. If you rent a commercial space for your business, your landlord may require you to carry some form of liability insurance.

Workers' compensation and disability insurance cover employees for loss of income and medical expenses as a result of job-related accidents. Many states require you to have workers' compensation insurance if you have employees.

Jeweler's block insurance is designed for most types of jewelry businesses. It covers risks faced by any business, like robbery, water damage, and fire, as well as risks that are industry-specific, like theft of jewelry stock, loss of customers' property, lost shipments, and much more. Optional insurance for jewelry on the road with a sales rep, at a trade show, or at an exhibition is also available.

Liability insurance is a necessity, and you may also want to consider getting jeweler's block insurance. An insurance broker can give you more information and help you decide what is best for you and your business.

BUSINESS PLANS

A business plan is a way to write down a statement of goals and your plans for reaching them. A business plan is for internal use, and it's also helpful in finding investors. Even if you are not looking for an investor, a business plan is crucial: it spells out what your vision and goals are.

Fill in the blanks on this business plan outline once a month and assess what worked, what didn't work, what you can change, and what your next move should be.

WHAT IS YOUR BUSINESS NAME?

_____

WHAT IS YOUR VISION FOR YOUR BUSINESS?

_____

What are your current, one month, one year, two year, and five year goals?

_____

What makes your business and jewelry unique?

_____

How do you plan to profit from your business?

_____

How do you plan to market your business?

_____

WHAT ARE THE STRENGTHS AND ADVANTAGES OF YOUR BUSINESS?

_____

What do you love doing when it comes to your business, and what are you good at?

_____

WHAT ARE THE WEAKNESSES AND DISADVANTAGES OF YOUR BUSINESS?

_____

What do you dislike doing when it comes to your business? What can you work around, learn to do, or find someone else to do?

_____

WHAT OPPORTUNITIES ARE THERE RIGHT IN FRONT OF YOU?

_____

List someone you've met, show you've heard about, awesome sale, new direction, new technology, etc. that can be an inspiration or help to your business.

_____

BUSINESS FINANCES

_____

What were your income and expenses this month? Did you have a profit or a loss? Where could you have spent less and made more money? What was your most profitable sale or experience?

_____

EVALUATION

_____

How has your vision evolved?

_____

How much profit did you make?

_____

How can you promote and market your jewelry line better?

_____

What opportunities are coming up next month?

_____

BUILDING A BRAND

Running a jewelry business is about much more than just jewelry. You are building a brand.

Business Name

Your business name is the first thing people see when they look at your product, and that should leave a good impression. Many artists and designers choose to design under their name, while others create a name that tells a story. When choosing a name, think about who you will be selling to. Think about how you will evolve and where your jewelry could take you. Pick something that is versatile and simple, and that people will remember.

When I first started my company, I launched it under the name *We Are Here*. I came from a background of fashion jewelry, where most labels sold under a cool and cryptic name. I felt funny using *Emilie Shapiro* to represent my jewelry because, frankly, I never liked my name. I wanted my business name to be powerful and impactful, something that told a story of everyday artifacts. But when galleries and museum shops started selling my work, they were confused. No one could remember the name *We Are Here*, so they just used my name instead. After the first two years, I rebranded my company as *Emilie Shapiro Contemporary Metals*. I decided to brand my line by my name to focus more on telling the story of an artisan-made product. My brand is about craftsmanship and celebrating beauty in imperfection. This was a great decision, as I have found people love to hear the artist's story and the inspiration behind my work.

Business Logo

A logo is a visual representation of your company (see example on page 11). There are three basic types of logos—font-based, a visual representation of what your company does, and an abstract graphic. A font-based logo would be just the company name in a specific font. A visual representation demonstrates what your company does, like an image of a piece of jewelry. An abstract graphic is like the Nike swoosh symbol or McDonald's arches.

Keep it simple and think about where it will be going. You want something that will look great printed on a large sign that is 2 feet (61 cm) wide, yet will still look clear printed on packaging that is 2 inches (5 cm) wide. Consider creating a dark and a light version to give yourself options when using it on marketing materials. If you're stumped about what to use for a visual logo, pay attention to what you are doodling next time your mind starts

wandering. All of us have an image we draw over and over again, and that may be a great way to visually represent you and your work.

Marketing and Promotional Materials

BUSINESS CARDS AND POSTCARDS

It is essential to have business cards, and lots of them. Carry your business cards with you at all times, and hand them out to everyone when you're speaking about your line. The card should have your company name and logo with your contact information, including your email address, phone number, and website. Consider creating a postcard with some beautiful pictures as a visual takeaway for a customer. On this kind of postcard, you can add more information about your jewelry, along with your contact information. Use the highest-quality resolution and the largest-size file of your images when incorporating them into a design for the best print quality. Check with the printer for size recommendations.

You don't have to spend a lot of money on business cards or postcards. Use a free template offered by an online printing company to create your marketing materials. Print them out yourself using thick card stock on a home computer, use a local print shop, or get them printed online. You can also design your marketing materials using design programs like InDesign and Adobe Photoshop. Although these programs are an expensive investment, you may get a lot of use out of them. For a less expensive option, you can purchase a cloud-based version of these design programs for roughly $10 a month.

ARTISTS' CARDS

Artists' cards are a great way to complement your jewelry by telling your story. In a succinct write-up, spotlight your inspiration, process, materials, and any other information you think the customer would like to know about your work. You can also include recommendations for jewelry care on the card. General jewelry care

involves avoiding harsh chemicals, like perfumes and chlorine, as well as keeping the jewelry from getting wet. Give instructions on how to clean the product by using a store-bought jewelry cleaner or another recommendation like warm water and mild dishwashing soap. Consider designing your artists' cards so they fit inside your jewelry packaging.

Customers love to hear about your inspiration and that helps sell your work. Artists' cards are a nice takeaway so the customer can remember and share the information if you are selling direct retail. This is a great addition to a wholesale order, too. Stores selling your jewelry can relay this information to their customers as an added bonus.

PHOTOGRAPHY

Good photography is extremely important for printed marketing materials, social media, websites, or for simple client emails. You can have the most fabulous designs, but if you have poor photographs of your work, no one will feel compelled to look further.

Good-quality product photography is vital in selling your work online. The most common method is to have your jewelry photographed on a clean white background. This is the easiest way to view products, and it is consistent with most other products being sold online. You can also consider shooting your images on a textured piece of paper or a piece of wood that complements your jewelry; just make sure to keep the backgrounds consistent. Press will often request high-resolution images on white backgrounds, so it is good to have these on file. The quality of images are measured in dots per inch, or dpi. If you zoom in really close to a photograph, the image consists of thousands of colored dots that create the picture. High resolution is 300 dpi or higher, and low resolution is anything lower than that. You will need high-resolution images for printed material, press and publication requests, and your website. Low-resolution images will be used to email photographs to keep your email from bouncing back.

With the right techniques, almost any camera can take good-quality images, even the camera on your smartphone. You can even purchase a lens to attach to your

smartphone to take better-quality images. You can find lens attachments starting at $20. Use a DSLR, or digital single-lens reflex, camera to shoot your jewelry. If you do not have one and cannot borrow one from a friend, you can rent a DSLR camera by the hour or the day from a photography studio or store.

The most important aspect of product photography is good lighting. For the most budget-friendly option, use natural light. Set up the products you want to photograph near a large window with good light streaming in. If this is hard for you to find, you can make your own light box by using a cardboard box, a box cutter, computer paper or white fabric, and tape. Cut at least a 4-inch-by-4-inch (10 cm x 10 cm) square out of all four sides and the

make sure to have the grid option turned on to help center your product.

You can edit images taken on your smartphone with the built-in editing program. You can easily edit the photographs taken on a DSLR camera yourself with a program like Lightroom, iPhoto, or Photoshop. Even if you are not an expert, adjust the tonal range and color balance levels and make sure the white background is the whitest point of the photo. You can also adjust the color saturation to intensify the hues of the piece. Crop your picture so the piece takes up about 80 percent of the frame, and the white background is about 20 percent. It is a good idea to save your unedited, raw files in two places, and save both large

top of the box, and leave the bottom fully intact. Adhere clean white fabric or paper to the openings that you made. This will help diffuse the light to give you consistent lighting and not create harsh shadows. Adhere a seamless piece of paper on the inside of your box from the top to the bottom. This is where you will set your pieces up to be photographed. No need for fancy lights: use clamp lights with daylight bulbs to light the outside of your light box from the top and sides. It is very important to place your camera or smartphone on a tripod so the distance between the camera lens and your piece is consistent, and to avoid shaky hands. When using your smartphone to take product photography,

files and smaller files of the edited versions. You will want to use the large files to create marketing materials and the small files to upload on your website and social media, and to email to clients.

If you do not want to edit the pictures yourself, use an inexpensive editing service like ClippingMagic.com. These services can edit your pictures for you and make the background completely white fast and inexpensively.

Find a photographer to take your product shots for you by contacting a photography store or studio, or list the freelance project on a job listing website. The best way to locate a quality photographer is by a referral, so ask around. Get in touch with a local college career center to find a student to do your photography for free or at a low cost in exchange for use in her portfolio. This is a great option if you do not want to spend a lot of money.

LINE SHEETS

Line sheets are a sales tool to give buyers all the vital information about your jewelry line (see example on page 16). Similar to a catalog, line sheets have images of all your products with their SKU (stock keeping unit), wholesale pricing, material information, and dimensions. Also include ordering information, like minimum opening order, minimum reorder, production time, and how to place an order. When approaching stores to ask

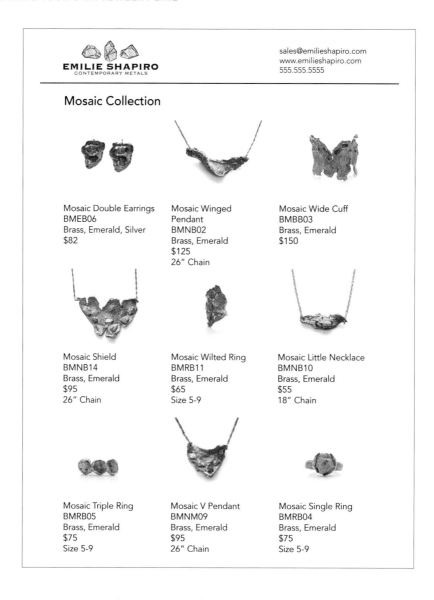

EMILIE SHAPIRO
CONTEMPORARY METALS

sales@emilieshapiro.com
www.emilieshapiro.com
555.555.5555

Mosaic Collection

Mosaic Double Earrings
BMEB06
Brass, Emerald, Silver
$82

Mosaic Winged
Pendant
BMNB02
Brass, Emerald
$125
26" Chain

Mosaic Wide Cuff
BMBB03
Brass, Emerald
$150

Mosaic Shield
BMNB14
Brass, Emerald
$95
26" Chain

Mosaic Wilted Ring
BMRB11
Brass, Emerald
$65
Size 5-9

Mosaic Little Necklace
BMNB10
Brass, Emerald
$55
18" Chain

Mosaic Triple Ring
BMRB05
Brass, Emerald
$75
Size 5-9

Mosaic V Pendant
BMNM09
Brass, Emerald
$95
26" Chain

Mosaic Single Ring
BMRB04
Brass, Emerald
$75
Size 5-9

them to carry your work, it is extremely important to have line sheets that clearly specify all information, including ordering information. Include your contact information on every page.

WEBSITE

Whether you have a Facebook page or a blog, a DIY website or a professionally built e-commerce site, it is imperative to have an online presence.

At the very least, begin with a Facebook page or a blog to share photographs of your work, inspirations, and upcoming event information. Use a free blog platform like Tumblr or WordPress to create a blog you can update right from your smartphone. This is a great idea when you are first starting to share your information. List your jewelry on third-party websites, like Etsy, Strolby, or Custommade, that already have a large audience coming to shop for products like yours. Design your own website using a template-based company like Squarespace, Domain.com, or GoDaddy, or have a site professionally built.

Read more about websites in the marketing section on page 97.

SOCIAL MEDIA

Social media is a highly effective way to build brand awareness and have customers discover you for free. Because there are so many platforms to choose from, and they are constantly changing and being updated, establishing a presence in social media can become overwhelming. Among the most popular platforms are Instagram, Facebook, Twitter, Tumblr, and Pinterest. Read more on social media in the marketing section on page 97.

JEWELRY BUSINESS PRACTICES

Like every business, the jewelry industry has its own language and ways of operating that you need to be aware of. If you are not sure what something is, ask for help or look it up.

Types of Jewelry Orders

COMMISSION PIECES AND ONE OF A KIND

Many jewelers work with clients one-on-one to create their dream piece. You may also create pieces that are one of a kind and have customers peruse them in person or online. This is a wonderful selling point because nothing else in the world is quite like this piece.

Creating handmade engagement rings, wedding bands, and bespoke jewelry is a great way to sell one-of-a-kind pieces. Post images on your social media outlets and your website so clients can see your past work. Clients may be interested in making an appointment with you to come see any ready-made pieces you have in person and speak with you about design. Set up a display area in your studio or workspace to meet with clients. If you don't have a designated space, meet clients at a coffee shop and bring your pieces or photographs of them with you. Take

down important information, like their ring size, contact information, and ideas they have for the potential piece. Follow up your meeting with an email reviewing everything you spoke about with some ideas to make working together easier. It is a good idea to get a 50 percent deposit when the order is placed; the balance will be due when the piece is complete.

Most commission work, especially wedding bands, will come by word of mouth. Ask your clients to write a review about their experience on a website like Yelp or Google Plus to help spread the word.

RETAIL

Retail is the selling of a product from a fixed location or an online shop, in small quantities or individual pieces, for direct consumption by the purchaser. You can retail your work at a variety of outlets—a private studio, a brick-and-mortar store, an online web store, a jewelry party, or a craft fair. Retail generally works well if you are pursuing your jewelry business part time, or supplementing your wholesale business with retail sales. Read more about retailing your work on page 107.

WHOLESALE

Wholesale is selling a product in large quantities to be resold by other retailers. A retailer is a person who will resell your work at the retail price at a brick-and-mortar shop, through a mail order catalog, or online at an e-commerce website. When you sell in bulk at a wholesale price to a store, it is important to establish a minimum order so it is worth your time and the discount on the goods you're extending to the shop owner. Read more about wholesaling your work on page 114.

WHOLESALE ORDERS

Physical stores, mail order catalogs, and websites purchase products in bulk at the wholesale price to sell to their customers. Find stores that might want to carry your work by looking locally in your area, getting recommendations from friends and customers, and at wholesale trade shows.

When approaching a store to ask them to carry your line, always do your research in advance. Buyers are very busy and you do not want to waste anyone's time if you are not a good fit for each other. Start by checking out local stores. See what products they carry and if your aesthetic and price point would complement the store's. Research other designers you think your work would sit well next to. Who do they sell to? Which other designers' work is carried at that store? Create a wish list of stores to carry your work and reach out to them at the beginning of a buying season. As you grow your wholesale business, you may look into exhibiting at a wholesale trade show to help market your line and find new accounts. If you are not interested or able to grow your sales by yourself, hire a sales representative or showroom. Read more about wholesale on page 114.

Purchase Orders and Invoices

A purchase order, or "PO," is a document from the buyer to the seller, stating what products and quantities the buyer wants to buy. Once the PO is accepted, a contract is drawn up between buyer and seller, specifying what is being ordered, the delivery date, and the agreed-upon price. When the order is shipped, the seller issues an invoice to the buyer, reflecting all the product and pricing information on the PO and stating the payment terms.

Wholesale accounts may call or email you with their purchase order. Depending on the store, they may have their own system to issue you a PO. Generally large stores like department stores and museum shops will have an ordering system in place. At a wholesale trade show, you will need to bring your own purchase order forms to write up when store buyers place orders in person.

Create a system to take orders and establish production times and ship dates before the show starts, so you won't be overwhelmed when you get your first order. Some stores want their order as soon as possible, or your first available ship date, and some want it at a specific time later in the year.

Buy a standard purchase order that has a carbonless copy underneath at your local office supply store. You will keep the top copy (usually white), and the buyer will take the carbon copy (usually yellow) for his records. Staple a business card to the buyer's copy so the buyer has all your information. As your business grows, you may want to consider creating a custom purchase order with your logo, contact information, and information that is tailored to make writing an order for your work easy.

Write neatly and clearly so you can understand the order when you get back to process it in your studio. Also make sure the buyer can read the carbon copy.

Many designers are gravitating toward paperless purchase orders. However, I feel that most buyers like a paper carbonless copy to take away for their records. You can write up an order on your computer and email it to the buyer to avoid using paper. Some systems use a scanner that scans the bar codes on your products to generate a purchase order.

SKU

A SKU (pronounced *skew*), or stock keeping unit, is a short code that refers to a specific product offered by a manufacturer. You can think of the SKU as your piece's nickname, instead of writing out the whole description. Each letter or number usually refers to a product type, material, size, color, and so on. It is important to give each piece a SKU because that makes ordering easier and faster. Most wholesale accounts will use your SKU number in their inventory system and will reference this when placing orders and reorders. Come up with a simple system to organize your products.

EXAMPLE: WFRB05-7

WF: Waterfall Collection. The first two letters represent which collection the piece is part of.

R: Ring. The third letter references the jewelry type.

B: Brass. The fourth letter represents the metal used in the piece.

05: The number the piece is in the collection.

7: This references the ring size. Different sizes or chain lengths can also be represented here.

Order Minimums

When you sell to a store in bulk at a wholesale price, it is important to establish a minimum order quantity so it is worth your time and the discount on goods the store is receiving. Your minimum can be a dollar amount or a piece amount. If a store is selling a collection of your work, encourage the buyer to order multiple pieces from the collection, rather than just one or two pieces. This way the retailer can display a collection of your work together, which looks better as a cohesive group and will sell better. If your work varies widely in price, consider establishing a piece minimum to avoid having a customer reach your minimum after just three pieces. If your price points are all relatively similar, a price minimum may work best for you. This is an industry standard, so don't feel shy requiring a minimum.

Price minimum: The retailer must order at least the minimum wholesale worth of merchandise to place an order. You may want to consider establishing a reorder minimum as well; however, some companies have no reorder minimums as an incentive for buyers to reorder.

Piece minimum: The retailer must order at least the minimum number of pieces from your collection for a wholesale order. This guarantees that the retailer will have an assortment of your work to merchandise in a group or throughout the store so customers can see the range of your work.

Payment Terms and Negotiating

When working with customers, you need to establish payment terms, sometimes referred to simply as "terms."

For custom retail orders, I recommend a 50 percent deposit, due when the order is placed, and the remaining 50 percent balance due when the piece is finished and the customer picks it up or it is shipped out.

For retail orders purchased online or in person, the customer should pay in full at the time the order is placed.

For wholesale accounts, there are a few different payment terms that may be used. I don't recommend extending payment terms to a first-time buyer. Instead, it's best to have the entire balance charged right before you ship.

Once you've established a relationship with a store, you may offer another payment term like Net30, where the invoice is due thirty days after the buyer receives the products. Accept this only if you are comfortable giving this store terms. Shipping your products before you have received payment should be done at your discretion. You can never be sure you will receive payment once you ship the items. On your purchase order and line sheets, clearly spell out your terms. I recommend adding a penalty for late payment, such as a 2 percent penalty charge for every day the payment is late.

If you work with expensive materials, you might want to take a deposit when the order is placed to give you some seed money to purchase supplies. Consider asking for a 10 percent deposit with the remaining balance due at the ship date. Be prepared for buyers, especially with larger department stores and museum shops, to refuse to pay a deposit. It is at your discretion if you choose to work with their own terms.

If you are writing up an order at a trade show, be sure to get the buyer's credit card information so you can charge the account upon shipping. This is an industry standard, so don't be shy about insisting on getting a credit card. Even if the buyer of the store wishes to use another form of payment when their order is charged, still take down a credit card number when taking an order. Consider creating a policy on your order form for cancelled orders. I suggest a 25 percent restocking fee if the order is cancelled ten or more days after the order was placed.

Larger accounts, such as mail order catalogs, department stores, and large e-commerce sites, will most likely have standard payment terms in place, like Net45, meaning you will get paid forty-five days from when they receive the products. Just remember that everything is negotiable and that confidence is key in business. If you feel uncomfortable with the terms, it doesn't hurt to ask for something else. The worst thing that will happen is that the buyer will say no.

Generally, larger accounts will offer a faster payment option with a discount like 2%Net10, meaning you will get paid within ten days from when they receive the products with a 2 percent discount.

Getting Paid

Create a designated area in your studio, like a file folder or a desktop tray, to keep open orders that are on net payment terms. Also mark the date each payment is due in your calendar so you know when to expect the payment. When the check arrives, or the buyer pays over the phone via credit card, mark her invoice as paid and file it with other paid orders. Keeping track of open orders is extremely important so payments don't fall through the cracks.

You can email the accounts payable contact and the buyer a reminder on the date their payment is due with their invoice attached. If you don't receive payment, pick up the phone and call your contact to remind him and see what is going on. Most of the time someone has forgotten, or there is a reason for the delay. Unfortunately, in a sluggish economy, sometimes Net30 can turn into Net60 or Net90.

If a customer has not paid you, reinforce your penalty policy, which should be written clearly on your line sheets and purchase order forms. You can file a report with your local Better Business Bureau, consumer affairs office, or, in some cases, your local chamber of commerce. Depending on the size of the outstanding balance, you can also file a claim with the small claims court in your area. You can go to small claims court yourself (that is, without a lawyer), or hire a lawyer to handle the matter for you. At best, this process is time-consuming; at worst, it's costly. If you get a lawyer involved, you will most likely pay more in legal fees and court costs than the total that's owed. Even if you win, sometimes you never collect. To avoid this, do not extend payment terms to new accounts or to stores that haven't been open long.

Accounting

Develop a clear accounting system for all payments coming in and all payments going out. I recommend using accounting software, like QuickBooks, FreshBooks, or Quicken, to generate your invoices and record income and expenses. Accounting software will help you keep track of sales tax you've collected, and you can run profit-and-loss statements and sales reports to help assess what is working and what isn't working in your business.

For quarterly or yearly taxes, you may figure out what's owed and file the forms yourself, use an online tax program, or hire an accountant. I recommend working with an accountant to file your taxes. By using a professional, you will ensure you are paying and filing at the right time to avoid additional fees.

Production

Depending on your designs, skills, and business model, you will need to establish who will be making your jewelry, how, and where. You may choose to create every piece from start to finish. Alternatively, you can contract out certain aspects of production, like casting, stone setting, and plating. Or you can have someone else make your entire collection from beginning to end.

IN-HOUSE PRODUCTION

For a small-scale production line, you may opt to make all the pieces in your own studio. Depending on your process and what equipment you need, you can set up a studio space in your home. This is ideal for processes like wax carving and light metalwork.

You can set up a studio space in a shared artists' building, a coworking space, or your own private art studio. Look for an established artists' building or commercial space to rent. Some jewelry studios rent the use of jewelry benches and equipment on an hourly, daily, or monthly basis, if you are not ready to commit to your own space.

As your business grows, you may need help keeping up with orders or freeing up your own time so you can focus on other aspects of running the business. Remember that growing pains are healthy, and they're a great problem to have. Try to focus on what aspects of the business you do best, and what you can delegate to someone else. Create a student internship program so you can have an extra set of hands, and your intern will learn about working with a small craft company. Contact a local college's career center and let the director know you have an internship to offer. Post an ad on websites geared toward craft and fashion internships, like ArtJobs or Barefoot Student. You can also use general job listing websites like Craigslist, LinkedIn, or Indeed. For more professional help,

hire a bench jeweler to work in your studio as a freelancer when you need the extra help, part time or full time. Contact a college or trade school with an art program or ask for referrals from other local jewelers.

CONTRACTING OUT

Depending on your skills and the volume of orders you have, you may choose to outsource some or all of your production. There is a huge jewelry industry worldwide with thousands of vendors who specialize in specific techniques. Most major cities have a jewelry district—some bigger than others—that can handle jobs large and small. Aim to keep your production as close to you as possible to better manage it. The farther away your production is from you, the more you risk miscommunication. Outsource work to a local industry. If vendors aren't available locally, most companies ship worldwide.

Read more about production on page 51.

Sourcing Materials

Whenever possible, buy materials in bulk at the lowest cost you can find. Get as close to the source as possible. If you are purchasing chain by the inch (cm) from a retail store, find a chain supplier and buy a larger quantity at a lower overall price to have the chain on hand. You can go in with other artists and friends to buy things in bulk you all use.

Establish what materials are essential to you and your brand, and find suppliers who share the same ethos as you. Certain materials and certifications may be important to you and also be used as selling points. If you make claims about a material or source, you will often be asked to show certificates verifying the authenticity of your claims if you are selling to a large retailer. As the designer and manufacturer, you are responsibile to make sure the claims you are making are accurate.

FAIR TRADE

Fair trade is a social movement to promote better trading conditions and sustainability in developing countries. Members of fair trade organizations promote higher wages and higher social and environmental standards. Many designers source fair trade gemstones to use in their products, and many customers seek them out. Be sure you are purchasing from a reliable source that is associated with a fair trade organization and can give you a certificate to go along with your purchase. You cannot market something as *fair trade* if it isn't certified.

RECYCLED METALS

Precious metals, like sterling silver and all alloys of gold, are easily recyclable. If you are interested in purchasing recycled metals, many vendors are now offering it in sheet, wire, and findings. If your jewelry is produced by lost-wax casting, check with your casting company to see if the company offers recycled metals. The company should be able to provide a certificate from its supplier to prove that its metals are recycled.

You may also want to check if the metal you are purchasing contains nickel. Many suppliers offer nickel-free metal because nickel is a common allergen. If you sell your products to large retailers and claim that your jewelry is nickel-free, you may need to prove that with a certificate that can be obtained by the supplier. Nickel and nickel compounds are one of the many chemicals covered by the State of California's Proposition 65, the Safe Drinking Water and Toxic Enforcement Act of 1986. Proposition 65 requires manufacturers to list all chemicals known to cause cancer in their products so the public can be aware that those products contain known carcinogens.

Even if you aren't planning to sell your jewelry in the state of California, you may want to consider purchasing metals that are manufactured without nickel.

CHAPTER 2

Learning about Jewelry Design

✦

There are many ways to learn about jewelry making. Know yourself and find which one works best for you. I suggest taking on small DIY projects first to gauge your interest. Jewelry-making equipment can be very expensive, so before you invest a lot of money, take some classes to learn the techniques and find your niche. Learning what you don't want to do is almost as important as learning what you do want to do.

As a craftsperson, you are constantly learning. Whether you gain knowledge by trial and error, by reading a book, or by taking a class, there are always new skills to learn. Living in the Internet age, we literally have the world at our fingertips. You can read a book, virtually take a class with a teacher in another country, or watch a real-time demo online. If you seek out information, you can find it.

DIY LEARNING

Trial and Error

One of the best ways to learn and hone your skills is by trial and error. Learn from your mistakes, and do it better and faster the next time. Select a project to work on and keep on practicing. Take notes while you work to assess how to change it the next time around. Look at jewelry with a critical eye and see how it is made. Take things apart and figure out how to put them back together.

While working as a bench jeweler in New York City's diamond district, I learned a great deal about making jewelry. Doing the same task over and over again, for eight hours a day, builds muscle memory, bolsters your bench skills, and makes you more proficient and faster. Some of our insiders talk about how they got started in jewelry making on page 137.

Books and Online Tutorials

Craft books are a great way to be inspired, to learn, and to perfect your skills. Find a book with easy-to-follow instructions and interesting projects to practice. Books are a great reference for basic techniques and resources, and are also inspirational, especially if they have beautiful pictures. Take notes while you're working on the project so you can look back to see what you've learned and how you can improve. Large bookstores like Barnes & Noble carry many craft books; so do small independent bookstores. You'll find a wide variety of books online at RioGrande.com and Amazon. Lessons online in PDF format are available from jewelry instructors, schools, and magazines.

Depending on how you learn, following a lesson through a book or PDF may or may not work for you. Some people are visual learners and need to see things in action to fully understand.

YouTube and DVDs

You can learn just about anything on You-Tube by typing into the search bar the skill you're looking to learn. Many PDF lessons come with a video lesson to follow along with, and many books come with a DVD tutorial. This is a great way to watch someone up close working with materials.

Downsides of learning like this are you can't ask the instructor a question and you have to purchase all the materials and equipment yourself.

INDIVIDUAL CLASSES AND COURSES

Small Studio Classes

A terrific place to begin to learn about designing and making jewelry is by enrolling in a class. Group classes are an excellent way to learn; you're not learning just from the instructor, but from the students around you. Taking a class at a jewelry studio is great because you can use shared equipment without having to buy expensive tools and materials. There are many independent jewelry studios that offer small group classes.

Many cities have class directories, like CourseHorse.com or MetalCyberspace .com, which list all the classes available and allow you to book online. Jewelry and craft magazines, such as *Metalsmith Magazine* and *Art Jewelry Magazine*, publish class directories as well. Jewelry guilds, such as the Society of North American Goldsmiths (SNAG), the Women's Jewelry Association (WJA), and the Enamelist Society, also have school directories and class resources.

Private Lessons

If you want to learn a specific jewelry-making technique, private lessons are ideal because the instructor can tailor the lesson to you. Contact a local jeweler or someone whose work you admire and see if he would be willing to give you a lesson or could recommend a teacher to you.

Although private lessons may be wonderful, I believe group classes are more conducive to learning because there is a curriculum for all students to follow and you learn a lot from the people around you. In a private lesson I find that students become too focused on the singular thing they want to learn and don't see the larger picture.

College-Level Classes

Check nearby colleges for jewelry-making classes and see if the college will allow you to enroll in one of them. College-level classes generally have outstanding faculty and equipment to learn on, and offer twelve-week classes.

Online Classes

Many schools offer online classes these days. You can see lessons in real time and ask the instructor questions while you're watching demos, and then rewatch the videos at your leisure. This approach is ideal when you're working with techniques that don't require many expensive tools and materials. Check out sites like Craftsy.com for short video classes and see what some of our insiders had to say about taking classes on page 154.

INSTITUTIONAL LEARNING

Trade School Programs

Consider a trade school if you want to pursue a technical education on how to fabricate metal, carve wax, set gemstones, and repair jewelry. Look into a certificate program if you are interested in working at a jewelry store or for a production company. Studio Jewelers in New York City and the Revere Academy of Jewelry Arts in San Francisco are both notable trade schools in the United States.

For training in gemstone and diamond grading, the Gemological Institute of

America, or GIA, is extremely well known and highly regarded in the jewelry industry. If you plan to work with and appraise diamonds, especially for engagement rings, or work with antiques, a GIA certification is an excellent idea. The GIA has campuses in New York City; Carlsbad, California; and eleven international campuses. It also offers a distance-learning program.

University Education

Consider getting your bachelor's degree at a liberal arts school with a solid jewelry and metalsmithing program. This will give you a broad education on craft and technique and access to other classes and programs throughout the university, like business and marketing.

Syracuse University, my alma mater, has a stellar jewelry program with state-of-the-art equipment and an outstanding faculty. My program focused on technique and craftsmanship, with an emphasis on design and experimentation. I was able to take business classes, as well as other things I was interested in, to gain a well-rounded education. The lessons covered the full sweep of history and classical and contemporary techniques, but allowed me to focus on areas of particular interest to me and work very closely with my professors.

Many colleges and universities have jewelry-design programs for which you just have to take a class or two, as well as two-year or four-year degree programs. Among notable jewelry-design programs at the college level in the United States are those offered by the Rhode Island School of Design (RISD), the Savannah College of Art and Design (SCAD), and the Fashion Institute of Technology (FIT).

REAL-LIFE EXPERIENCE

Internships and Apprenticeships

A great way to learn and expand your skills is to apprentice with an artist or do an internship at a company. Not only will you see the artist's design process close at hand, but, more importantly, you'll learn how a business works from the ground up. Nothing can replace real-world experience. Ask local artists if they could use your help in exchange for learning. Check with your local jewelry-making school or university to see if they know of any alumni offering internship programs. Websites like Internsushi.com, LinkedIn.com, and Fashionista.com have listings for internships.

Reach out to a designer whose work you love and would like to learn from. Research the designer's work before contacting her. Write a well-thought-out email or place a phone call to her once you know exactly how you'd like to approach her. Explain what you admire about her work, what skills you can offer, and what you are looking to learn from her. This is a great way to learn how to make jewelry and to learn about the business behind it.

Working in the Industry

If you are looking to learn more about the jewelry business and jewelry design, consider trying to work in the jewelry industry to get some experience. There are many aspects of the business where you can work, either part time or full time. Look for jobs as a sample maker to learn about assembly and beading, a bench jeweler to refine your bench skills, or in sales and marketing to gain valuable insights into building your own jewelry business. Look for a job at a jewelry store in sales to gain merchandising, customer service, and sales experience. Working in the industry can be a great learning experience and also help you underwrite your own business.

You may find it hard to be inspired or find the time to design and make your own jewelry, since your creative energy is going into someone else's work. You may also have to abide by a non-compete clause while you're working for someone else,

depending on the company. A non-compete clause is a contract where you agree to not design or work for a similar company in competition with your current employer. Depending on the clause, you may be asked to not design or create your own jewelry on the side while working at the employer.

Look at local job listings to find a job in the jewelry industry. You can approach a local jeweler or an artist whose work you admire to see if they have any openings. You can also look into using a headhunter who focuses on design-based jobs.

PROFESSIONAL DEVELOPMENT

Consider learning about other programs and techniques that will help you become a better designer and business owner.

Design Programs

Read a book, or take a class in design programs like Photoshop and InDesign. These will be highly useful when you're designing marketing materials. Both are relatively user-friendly and have a lot of tutorials to help you navigate their functions, although these programs are extremely expensive. To save some money, use a cloud-based system.

Consider learning about photography and photo-editing programs. Most computers come with a photo-editing program for easy touch-ups, like changing the color balance and saturation, and cropping images. Taking good photographs of your jewelry is crucial for marketing and will be helpful if you have the skill set and equipment to do it well. Read more about photography on page 12.

Computer-aided design, or CAD, is a program used to design two- and three-dimensional representations of an object. This is now widely used in the jewelry industry and many other industries, and many large companies are using this to make their prototypes. You can find studio and college-level courses on CAD for jewelry; however, the computer programs are very expensive. Once your CAD file is designed, it can be 3-D printed in a wide variety of materials. Get your models printed at a 3-D printing company like Shapeways. They also have designers on staff to help you design your model. It is extremely useful to know the program if you plan to work in the jewelry industry or design your prototypes in CAD.

Business Classes

I highly recommend reading up on basic business practices or taking an Introduction to Business class to help navigate the waters. You don't have to have a master's in business administration, but it will be helpful to know how things operate in business and the lingo to go along with it.

CHAPTER 3

Design for Production

✦

TYPES OF DESIGN

One of a Kind

Creating jewelry pieces with no two alike takes a special talent, and becomes a big selling point. Customers may be on the lookout for one-of-a-kind pieces. One-of-a-kinds sell very well at craft markets and online. Some wholesale accounts, usually galleries, look for one-of-a-kind pieces, but it may be hard to scale a business up offering only one-off pieces.

Commission

Certain customers love working directly with the artist to create the perfect piece, customized just for them. This works especially well when designing wedding, engagement, and other bespoke jewelry. Many customers seek out a local designer to design and create the ideal piece. Ask commission clients to recommend you to others through word of mouth or by writing a review online. Invite customers to make an appointment with you at your studio, or meet at a coffee shop to discuss ideas.

Limited Edition

Depending on what materials you are using, you may only be able to make, or choose to release, only a specific number of pieces. If you are working with vintage parts or rare gemstones, for example, quantities may be limited. Consider numbering each piece by engraving directly into the metal, adding a tag or a label with the number the piece is in the edition. Limited-edition pieces sell well to retail buyers at craft markets and online. Some wholesale accounts will be interested in limited edition if they are purchasing only a small number of pieces. Most large wholesale accounts, however, like a department store, catalog, or website, shy away from limited editions because they need large quantities and the ability to restock.

Production

Production jewelry is meant to be made over and over again. This can be for a small scale—that is, tens of pieces—or large scale, meaning hundreds or even thousands of pieces. Design your pieces so they are easy to re-create by perfecting the design in your model, or first piece. Break your production steps down and focus on efficiency over design. Production jewelry will sell well to both retail and wholesale channels.

COSTUME JEWELRY

Traditionally referred to as "paste jewelry," costume jewelry is made from base metals and inexpensive or synthetic stones, and is sometimes plated with a precious metal. Oftentimes, the components are simply assembled, not soldered or otherwise secured in place.

BRIDGE JEWELRY

Bridge jewelry is generally created from sterling silver and semiprecious gemstones. These days, more designers are using brass and bronze in bridge jewelry as the price of precious metals rises, and more customers are interested in purchasing it.

FINE JEWELRY

Fine jewelry incorporates precious metals, like all alloys of gold, palladium, and platinum, and precious gemstones, such as diamonds, sapphires, and rubies. More designers are pushing the limitations of what is defined as "precious" by mixing materials of different values and featuring more unusual gemstones like raw diamonds, opal, colored beryl, and other stones less commonly used in commercial fine jewelry.

DESIGN TYPES

RINGS

When designing rings, you need to make them both functional and comfortable. If you make your rings too chunky, the customer can't close her fingers. If your rings are too thin, they'll be flimsy and won't hold their shape. The inside of each ring has to be smooth and comfortable. Most importantly, make sure your ring sizes are correct. Invest in a good-quality ring mandrel, which is calibrated with ring sizes, to check that your designs are the correct size. Also have a ring gauge on hand, whether you're at a retail or a wholesale show, or are working with a client in your studio. A ring gauge is a full set of rings in every size, including half sizes.

Some designers make adjustable rings, where the back is open and the customer can open or close it to their specific size, but this is generally offered only in costume jewelry. Standard United States ring sizes are 5 through 9 for women, and 8 through 11 for men. The most popular sizes are size 7 for women and size 9 for men. For a smaller or larger size, most likely you will be fulfilling a custom request. Use the most common sizes when creating a set of samples. I have found that if customers can't get a ring on, they generally won't purchase it, whether they're buying for retail or wholesale. Establish a ring resizing policy for both retail and wholesale orders. If you offer free ring sizing, that will encourage a customer to purchase the piece with the confidence that they can wear it.

NECKLACES

When designing necklaces, keep sizing and chain lengths in mind. Standard chain lengths include choker (14" [35.5 cm]), princess (16" [40.5 cm]), standard or matinee (18" [45.5 cm]), opera (20" [51 cm]), and lariat (30" [76 cm]). Remember that every necklace length will look different on every person depending on their shape and size. Consider making your necklaces with a chain extension, so customers can choose between the shorter and longer length, depending on which link they attach to the clasp.

Make sure your necklace closures are secure but also easy to take on and off. Every part of your necklace design should be softened and smoothed to avoid angry customers whose clothing is snagged by your piece.

EARRINGS

The most important thing to keep in mind when designing earrings is to make sure they are very secure. Your earring can have a post, or a thin hardened wire, to go through the ear and be secured by an earring back. For more movement, your earrings may have an earring wire, or J-hook. I recommend offering plastic earring backs as an option for extra security with earring wires. Some designers make clip-on earrings for people who don't have pierced ears or can no longer wear pierced earrings. Keep in mind that customers won't be able to wear your earrings if they are too heavy.

BRACELETS

There are three basic types of bracelets—cuffs, bangles, and charm bracelets.

Cuffs are open in the back and are usually more of an oval shape so they comfortably fit your wrist. Some cuffs are pliable enough that customers can adjust them to the wrist. The average diameter, or measurement if you draw a straight line across the middle of the cuff, is 2½ inches (6.5 cm). The opening in the back is usually 1 inch (2.5 cm) wide so customers can adjust it to their own fit.

A bangle is a continuous circle that is large enough to slide over the wrist, but small enough not to fall off. Sizing for bangles can be tricky, since hand size and wrist size vary greatly. The average diameter, or measurement if you draw a straight line across the middle of the bangle, is between 2 inches (5 cm) and 2½ inches (6.5 cm). You may consider having a small and a large bangle size, or just going with a standard size of 2¼ inches (5.5 cm).

Charm bracelets are made of a flexible material, like chain or rope, and are secured around the wrist with a clasp. The bracelet can range between 6 and 8 inches (15–20.5 cm), with the average size 7 inches (18 cm). You may consider having a chain extension for sizing options, offering different sizes, or just going with the standard size.

DESIGNING A COLLECTION
Finding Inspiration

Inspiration is everywhere. Humans have always had a primal urge to create something and leave their mark by reflecting on their surroundings or reflecting within themselves. In today's world, we are constantly flooded with images, both online and offline. When looking for inspiration for your jewelry line, come up with your own take on life and the world around you. It is often said that no idea is entirely original, since we are all inspired by the same themes. Find your own style by experimenting with different tools and techniques, and by repetition and practice.

THEMES

Throughout history, many themes have inspired artists and others—nature and natural elements, architecture and shapes, astrology and astronomy, culture and people, and color and texture. Look for inspiration everywhere and collect images or make sketches of things you are drawn to.

BOOKS, MAGAZINES, AND BLOGS

Look for inspirational images from the past and the present to help establish the mood of your jewelry designs. You'll find countless books about modern and antique jewelry, but also turn to shapes, art, nature, and symbols for inspiration. Check out runway shows for lines and color for the upcoming season, and peruse magazines for the latest fashion trends. Look at blogs for images drawn from art, architecture, fashion, and nature.

MUSEUMS

Visit museums for inspiration through historical and modern art. Many museums have collections of jewelry. I love studying the incredible permanent collection at the Museum of Art and Design in

New York City. The museum has jewelry on display that is thousands of years old, modern-day work, and pieces in between.

TECHNIQUE

Find inspiration by learning and practicing various jewelry-making techniques. Many artists are inspired by their process and the results they achieve. Study ancient jewelry techniques, like granulation, keum-boo, and mokume gane, and draw inspiration through trial and error. Many artisans highlight a specific technique in their work.

CREATE A MOOD BOARD

A mood or inspiration board is fun to make, and a great exercise to jump-start a collection. Collect all your ideas—sketches, images, objects, or clippings from magazines—and arrange them on a piece of paper or a corkboard. Pull shapes, colors, and themes from your mood board to see all your inspirations in one place. I like to hang my inspiration board above my desk so I'm constantly looking at it, as I add and take away things to help figure out the next direction for my line.

Create an inspiration board online by using a website like Pinterest. You can upload images, pin them from any website, or follow other people to see what they are adding. This is a terrific way to organize all your inspirations on the go.

FIND YOUR NICHE

When finding inspiration for a collection and designing jewelry, work on developing your own look. Although it is not always intentional, no one likes a copycat. Think about what will set you apart from other designers so you can develop your own style.

FOUNDATIONS OF A MARKETABLE COLLECTION

Whether you are starting from scratch or have created hundreds of pieces, making a jewelry collection is very different from designing just one piece. Designing a collection is about translating one design into many different forms of jewelry. If you designed a ring, translate that into a necklace, earrings, and a bracelet. Keep in mind that every customer will gravitate toward a certain type of piece. Some people love rings and that is all they buy. Other customers want pieces that go together. Buyers for a wholesale account may want to present the full collection so there is something for everyone.

Practice taking one of your designs and translating it into a collection. Start with one shape, color scheme, or texture, and translate that into all forms of jewelry. Create high, medium, and low price point items. The high, or reach, pieces, will draw customers in. These are real showstoppers—your statement necklace or cuff, for instance. The medium pieces will be the core items in your collection. The low pieces, or upsell items, are easy add-ons that sell quickly, like simple earrings or pendants. Practice taking a shape, gemstone, or texture, and design a collection with high, medium, and low pieces in all forms of jewelry. This exercise will make you a better designer.

Aim to design ten pieces in your first collection. As time goes on, redesign pieces to make them more functional and salable, edit out pieces that do not sell, and add pieces by expanding on what worked.

Here's a simple way to expand your collection: change the color or stone type, or offer another color of metal or finish. This is an easy and effective approach to building a strong and cohesive twenty-piece collection.

At the first wholesale trade show where I showed my designs, all my samples were made to fit my tiny wrists and fingers so I could wear my samples. I quickly learned that customers will not place orders if they cannot fit into your jewelry. Keep in mind standard sizing when making your jewelry samples. If customers can't slip on your pieces, most likely they will not order any of them. Create your ring samples in size 7, the most common female ring size, and make sure your bracelets fit most people.

For that first trade show, I didn't have a cohesive collection, but simply a grouping of random pieces I had created since I first started making jewelry. Designing rings has always come naturally to me, so rings comprised half of my display; everything else was a mishmash of other forms of jewelry. Buyers loved my rings but wanted to see what else went with them. Although I had some good designs, some of which are still part of my line, I didn't present a cohesive collection.

Design Schedule

Create a design schedule around seasonal markets. At first, aim to create two collections a year—one for spring/summer and one for fall/holiday.

If you are selling to craft markets and to retail sites online, your biggest season with always be in the late fall to holiday. For most designers, 50 percent of their sales come from the holiday season. Most people are looking for gift items at that time of year, so they have a legitimate reason to buy, and not just to splurge. Sales will most likely also be up just before Valentine's Day and Mother's Day, and at outdoor shows in the summer. As you build a following, the goal is for the customers to come back to make additional purchases and see what is new. Although it is not imperative to debut new collections, it is a good habit to get yourself in if you plan to expand into wholesale one day.

If you are selling your work wholesale, be aware that jewelry sales are cyclical and buying is sometimes done a whole season ahead, as it is in all of fashion. Depending on the store, some buyers will order for immediate shipment since, unlike clothing, jewelry rarely changes with the seasons. Establish a design schedule at the beginning of the year and stick to it. Even if you aren't exhibiting at a wholesale trade show, reach out to buyers at the beginning of the buying season. In the middle or toward the end of the buying season, many buyers will have used up their whole budget for the season or already met their quota of a category your work fits into.

If you don't stick to your design schedule and you don't come out with new products for each season, you will miss out on sales. If time is running short and inspiration is running dry, update old styles easily by changing the color, finish, or gemstone.

Many designers give each collection and product a name. This gives the collection character and can be used for marketing purposes. Collection names help establish an overall theme, and each product name tells a story that advances an ongoing narrative about your collection. Don't feel pressured to come up with names for your pieces. It's perfectly fine to call something a sapphire ring.

HOW TO SCHEDULE YOUR WORK FLOW

January/February: Jewelry designers show their spring collections at trade shows. Many jewelry lines will feature online and in-person sales to get rid of excess holiday inventory. Stores are replenishing inventory after the holiday season. Smaller boutique stores may be looking for spring inventory shipping out March and April. Larger stores may be looking to pull samples for summer inventory for May delivery.

March/April: Focus on production of spring orders and arranging sample pulls and returns with larger stores. Create samples for your new collection to promote in May and June. Photograph, price, and update your line sheets.

May/June: Jewelry designers show their fall collections at trade shows. Some designers choose to skip showing a new collection during this time, as it is the smallest season. If you are exhibiting at a wholesale trade show, keep in mind that stores may not have events at this time of year. Smaller stores may order summer inventory or reorder merchandise from spring. Larger stores may be looking to pull samples for fall inventory to be shipped in July.

Late June/July: Designers will create samples for holiday collections to promote in August and September. Photograph, price, and update your line sheets. Larger stores will also be planning their orders for holiday inventory in June and July to be shipped in September. Holiday orders are generally much larger than those placed during the rest of the year, sometimes even twice as large, so make sure to prepare to ramp up your production.

August/September: Jewelry designers exhibit their holiday/winter collections at trade shows. Send in applications for holiday craft fairs and make plans with hosts for jewelry parties and trunk shows for the holiday season. Smaller stores are stocking up on inventory for fall and holiday shipping in October and November. Larger stores are looking to pull product samples for the winter season shipping out in January.

October/November: Consider selling your work at jewelry parties, trunk shows, and/or holiday craft fairs for the season. Focus on production of fall and holiday orders and arranging sample pulls and returns with larger stores. Your orders will most likely go up in size and volume for retail and wholesale at this time of year.

December: Finish shipping out holiday orders through the end of the month. Take a break. You probably need and deserve one by now! Create samples for your spring collection to show in January and February. Photograph, price, and update your line sheets.

Merchandise

Before you can sell your work, you need to make sure your pieces are both functional and comfortable. Market-test your products by wearing them and lending them to friends. This is one of the best ways to get feedback. Your jewelry should look amazing when someone wears it, feel great, and

wear well. Make sure it is easy to put on and take off but is still secure. Your work should have no sharp areas or pieces that are uncomfortable. Be open to criticism, listen to what everyone says, and see how you can improve your designs.

Analyze and evaluate your collections after every season. What were your best-selling pieces? How can you expand on those best sellers in the form of new products? Perhaps you had a gemstone that was exceedingly popular. Can you come up with other designs incorporating that stone or a complementary palette to enhance that collection?

What pieces did not do well? That is, which had lackluster sales or serious production issues? Discontinue styles that didn't work and put the remainder of your inventory of that style on sale. If a piece has a design flaw, see if you can work out the kinks by adjusting the size or making it more comfortable, and reintroducing it.

PRICING YOUR JEWELRY TO SELL

When pricing your jewelry, remember that your goal is to make money. This is what will set you apart from hobbyists and designers who can't make their business work. Whether this is your part-time or full-time job, you need to get paid for your designs and the work that goes into it.

Too often I see designers selling their work at retail craft markets or online for much less than products in the same category. You may feel funny at first asking someone to shell out some cash, but remember you are offering a handmade, well-made product. Although you may feel that you can sell more with a low-priced item, you are putting in a lot of time and resources to create those products. This is not a sustainable business practice for the long term, and you won't be able to grow your business if you don't make a profit.

If a store notices you and wants to place a wholesale order, you then have to cut your retail prices in half, and you'll lose money if you didn't price your pieces correctly. Even if you are not planning to sell wholesale, always generate your retail price from a wholesale price to leave room for options and growth in the future.

Pricing for Your Market

A little research goes a very long way, so research possible retail outlets in your immediate area. Take a walk around your area to see what the shops are selling. Who are the customers of those shops and what is their typical price point? Can you see your work being sold there? Many small shops promote locally made and handmade goods. Look for handmade jewelry on display that you think your work would sell well next to. Research where else that designer sells, which designer's work is showcased next to his, and how much his work costs. How does your jewelry compare to those designers' in terms of price? Look online for other jewelry using similar materials as yours in a comparable market. How does your price compare to theirs?

After you price your products, compare them to other prices in your market. If your prices are too low, you know you can raise them a little. If your prices are too high, consider lowering them so as not to shut yourself out.

Who is your target demographic? Are you sure? Retail craft shows are an amazing way to market-test products to see if prices work, what people are gravitating toward, and who is buying. When I established my line, I was sure my target demographic was an urban, chic eighteen- to twenty-five-year-old with a love for fashion and interesting accessories. I was dead wrong. When I began doing retail shows and marketing my work online, my main demographic was forty-five-plus with a love for handcrafted, unusual, and eco-friendly items. It took me many years to realize that you can't fight the demographic. Those in the forty-five-plus demographic have a few hundred dollars to spend on a piece of jewelry, while the eighteen- to twenty-five-year-olds generally don't.

Pricing Formula

The basic formula below is a great tool to use to loosely price your jewelry. The reason I say *loosely* is that I like to use the formula, and then compare the price I come up with to pieces by other designers in the same price point and adjust. Where are you selling these pieces and who are you selling them to? And how does the price compare to other pieces sold in the same category? Make sure your pieces fit comfortably in the category—they shouldn't be too expensive or too cheap. Who is your target demographic, and does your pricing make sense for these prospective customers? After pricing a piece, ask yourself, "Would I pay that price for that piece?" If the price is too high or too low, adjust it. Look online at websites that sell a wide variety of jewelry to compare pricing.

THE MOST BASIC FORMULA TO USE:
Materials + Time = Cost x 2 =
Wholesale x 2 = Retail

When using this formula, there are four important numbers we are going to get— base, cost, wholesale, and retail. You can use the most basic version, or the more complex breakdown below.

PRICING FORMULA BREAKDOWN:
Base price = (Model + Mold) / Number of pieces you plan to sell (for example, 5)
Cost = (Base price + Materials + Labor) x 10%
Wholesale = Cost x 2
Retail = Wholesale x 2.2

BASE PRICE
A base price is the amount you need to charge for every piece sold to account for the amount spent while creating the first piece. If you have a model, or your master piece, you have to pay for that, too. Remember, you also paid for materials and spent time inventing and creating this piece. If you contracted work out, factor that in here. If you carved a piece in wax, factor in your labor for the hours it took. If you have a mold, apply that cost here. Even though these don't go into every finished production piece, you still need to pay for them. If you are positive you'll absolutely sell ten pieces, divide by ten. If you think you'll sell five pieces, divide by five.

COST
The cost is the amount it costs you, including materials and labor, to create the specific piece. This number is extremely

important to have so you know how much profit you're making on this piece in both wholesale and retail, and how much wiggle room you have to offer a discount in the future while still making a profit. To calculate your cost, add together your base price, materials, and labor. Don't shortchange yourself when it comes to your labor. This is an expert skill, which someone is paying for. You should be paying yourself at least $15 an hour and give yourself a raise as you feel your skills improve. If you are still learning, and making pieces takes you longer than an industry expert, your customer shouldn't pay for that. Don't forget to factor in your overhead. Overhead accounts for the everyday costs that keep your business up and running. These costs include studio rent, utilities, and anything else you pay monthly or yearly to keep your business afloat. I like to add 10 percent to the initial cost to factor in for overhead. Knowing your cost will help you in the long run: you'll know how much you can discount a piece for wholesale, retail, and sales reps while still making a profit.

WHOLESALE

This price is used when wholesale accounts are purchasing your work. Generate this number by multiplying your cost by at least two. Even if you are not planning to wholesale your work right away, it is important to figure this number in your pricing. If you don't calculate for wholesale and go right to retailing your work, you will be undercharging. If you get a wholesale account in the future, you won't be making any money from your jewelry.

RETAIL

This price is used when selling your jewelry to retail channels online and in person. Most retailers mark up wholesale between 200 percent and 250 percent, depending on their customers. Average markup is 220 percent, so generate your retail price by multiplying your wholesale by 2.2.

You may consider establishing an MAP, or minimum advertised price. This is a great idea, especially if you sell your work online. You shouldn't compete with other outlets and you want to avoid having someone undersell your work. I recommend establishing a 220 percent MAP policy, sometimes simply called a 2.2 MAP policy, which is the industry average. Make your MAP policy clear on your line sheets and order forms to avoid confusion with buyers.

Cutting Costs to Make a Larger Profit

Make sure you can make money from your designs. If your products are turning out to be outrageously expensive and no one will pay for them, how can you lower the cost?

First, see how you can lower the cost of your materials. Look for another source, ask for price breaks when buying in bulk, or consider a less expensive option without compromising quality too much. If you are working with precious metals, try to make your pieces lighter, so you use less metal and lower your cost. Try hollowing out your piece from the inside to make the metal weigh less, but still have the same aesthetic. This technique works great on the inside of rings and bracelets, and the backs of earrings and necklaces. Perhaps your labor expenses are too high. If you are doing the labor yourself, maybe it is taking you too long and someone else could do it faster and cheaper. This will free up your time to focus on other aspects of the business. If you are using outside contractors, ask for price breaks if you boost your production or try to find someone who will do the job for less.

CHAPTER 4

Producing Your Collection

✦

Now that you have designs, it's time to create your jewelry. Think about where you will be designing and producing your jewelry line, and who will be doing it. You may be making every piece yourself, have help from an intern or assistant, contract out certain aspects of production, or have all your production contracted out. Set your business up to grow, adopt good habits, and learn about all aspects of the jewelry industry.

Have a designated set of samples for your collections. These samples should be an exact replica of the pieces in your production line. Never sell these pieces, so you can reference them for production, display them for client meetings and wholesale trade shows, send them out on press pulls for fashion shoots, and use them for photography.

STOCK AND INVENTORY

You can either have stock pieces on hand or make your pieces to order. This depends on what type of jewelry you make and what materials you are using. If your jewelry incorporates expensive raw materials, like gold and precious stones, consider making your pieces to order. If you are using less expensive materials, you can build some stock to have on hand to sell. If you plan to sell your work at craft fairs and other events, you need to build an inventory to replenish as pieces sell. Start by making two of each piece, and see which pieces sell first. Once one piece sells, replace it with two more. Over time you will see what pieces are most popular and stock more of them. If you are focusing on wholesale, making pieces to order may work better for your line, since you will see the order before you need to fill it.

CREATE SYSTEMS THAT WILL GROW WITH YOU

For all my internal information including design specs, inventory management, and production schedules, I use a cloud-based system, like Google Drive or Evernote. I run this program on my computer, which also connects to my smartphone. All this information is backed up on a hard drive, just in case anything ever goes wrong. This works well for me because I can access the information anywhere and share it with my employees to use on their devices. This also cuts down on the amount of paper that we use in the studio.

Processing Orders

Develop a clear system to keep track of your orders. From the moment you accept a purchase order, you need to have a system in place to respond to that order in a timely manner. You'll have to place an order for materials, produce the products, and pack and ship merchandise.

When orders are placed, have a designated spot to record them. You can use a bulletin board by your desk, an order book, or a computer file to keep everything in order by ship dates. Also have a designated calendar where you enter ship dates and other deadlines. You don't want to be late on ship dates and tarnish your relationship with your accounts.

Master Production List

Create a master production list to organize every piece of information about every piece in your line. If you start this from the beginning, it will be easy to keep up with and save you lots of time when searching for information. Use a spreadsheet, with each column dedicated to information like SKU, product name, materials, dimensions, mold number, type of chain and chain length, wholesale cost, retail cost, and so on. Each row will represent a different product in your line. I find this extremely helpful when customers ask me for product information. It takes me just a few minutes to respond to their requests, since I already have dimensions and descriptions on file. Since everything is online in my cloud-based system, I can access it anywhere and get what I need. This comes in handy when I'm at my caster, placing an order, and need mold numbers; at a trade show and need to

MASTER PRODUCTION LIST

SKU	Product Name	Description	Mold Number	Metal	Chains/ Findings	Gemstone	Dimensions	Cost	Wholesale	Retail MAP
TCRB01	Triangle Ring	Trillian-cut sapphire is bezel set in recycled brass, showcased on a sterling silver ring shank. Available in whole sizes 5-9.	ES001— triangle setting	brass, sterling silver	16 g sterling silver round wire, fabricated to form simple ring	7 mm x 7 mm x 7 mm trillian-cut cornflower blue sapphire	.5" Length x .5" Width x .75" Height	$43	$86	$189
TCEB02	Triangle Earrings	Trillian-cut sapphire is bezel set in recycled brass, dangling from sterling silver earring wires	ES001— triangle setting	brass, sterling silver	20 g sterling silver french earring wires (2)	7 mm x 7 mm x 7 mm trillian-cut cornflower blue sapphire	.5" L x .5" W x 1.5" H (from earring wire)	$62	$124	$272
TCNB03	Triangle Necklace	Trillian-cut sapphire is bezel set in recycled brass, anchored from an 18" sterling silver cable chain.	ES001— triangle setting	brass, sterling silver	18" 1.5 mm sterling silver cable chain. One 5 mm lobster clasp, two 3 mm round split jump rings	7 mm x 7 mm x 7 mm trillian-cut cornflower blue sapphire	.5" L x .5" W x 18" H	$48	$96	$212
TCBB04	Triangle Bracelet	Trillian-cut sapphire is bezel set in recycled brass, delicately placed on a sterling silver bangle.	ES001— triangle setting, ES002— simple bangle	brass, sterling silver	no additional chains/ findings	7 mm x 7 mm x 7 mm trillian-cut cornflower blue sapphire	.5" L x .5" W x 3" D	$71	$142	$312

reference a SKU; or away from my studio and need dimensions and descriptions to send to a customer.

Spec Sheets

For each piece, make a spec sheet with details about the piece, including materials, dimensions, and every step involved in making it. These will be helpful when you're teaching a bench jeweler how to make your pieces or communicating with outside vendors on how something should look. A spec sheet should have an image of your piece, along with material information and how to create it from start to finish. Include information like mold numbers, sizing, stone information, chain length, and patinas. Consider photocopying each piece and then adding the information on the photocopy. Photocopies work very well, especially if you are fabricating each piece and need to reference sizing and templates.

Inventory

Keep track of your inventory by using a spreadsheet. In the far-left column, list every

SPEC SHEET

SKU: TCRB01

Product Name: Triangle Ring

Production Instructions:

- Fabricate plain ring from 18 g sterling silver round wire. Cut wire, file edges, form, and solder with hard solder.

- Size 5: 49.2 mm | Size 6: 52.4 mm | Size 7: 55.6 mm | Size 8: 58.7 mm | Size 9: 61.9 mm

- Clean casting of brass bezel. Cut sprue, grind, sand.

- Solder brass casting to sterling silver ring. File gentle flat edge on ring to prep for soldering on original solder seam. Place bezel face down on charcoal block. Using third arm, hold silver ring with cross lock tweezers perpendicular to bezel. Check angles are correct from top and side views. Solder using hard solder.

- Give ring final sand with 600-grit sandpaper. Tumble.

- Send finished pieces to be set at stonesetter.

---

product in your line. In the next column, record how many of each style you have in stock. Your inventory should include raw materials and finished jewelry. Each time you sell something, reduce your inventory accordingly, so you can see what and how many pieces you need to make to replenish your supply. Do an inventory check periodically and record your amounts in the appropriate column: you can do this once a week, once a month, before a show, or whatever works for your business. This is a great tool when restocking inventory and designing a new collection. You can see what styles, colors, and sizes sell better or worse compared to the others.

You can also combine your inventory spreadsheet and your production list, if you plan to use just one. This will consolidate information and save you time so you don't have to repeat writing things down.

SETTING UP A STUDIO SPACE

Regardless of where you set up your studio—and whether it's big or small, part time or full time—start with the essentials and don't spend a lot of money all at once. Try to purchase as many of your tools and as much of your equipment as you can used. These should be good quality and in good condition, but they're less expensive than if you bought them new. Even if you have a small space, establish two essential areas in your studio—dirty and clean. Your dirty area may be your jeweler's bench, where you do metalwork, soldering, resin work, or anything else that's messy. Your clean area may be for wax carving, packing and shipping, and office work. Expand on these areas as you need more space.

Home Studio

Depending on your process and what equipment you need, you can set up a studio space in your home. This works well for processes like wax carving and light metalwork. Make sure to have good ventilation if you are using resins, patinas, or other toxic chemicals. At the very least, put an exhaust fan in your window, drawing the air outside.

Check your municipality's laws about having a gas tank in a residential space. Usually the fire department can point you in the right direction or let you know the regulations and what licenses are needed to own and operate certain types of gas tanks.

Some people find that working from home is ideal, but it's not for everyone. This may be a great setup for you if you are making jewelry part time, so you can maximize the time you spend on your jewelry. If you are focusing on design and using outside contractors to produce your jewelry, a home office setup may work well. Certain jewelry makers work better in a space outside their home, so they can easily separate their business and personal life.

Shared Artists' Studio

You can rent a shared artist space in a commercial building for your studio. Many jewelry designers love this kind of shared space because artists can share ideas and tools and build a strong community together. Look for a space in established art buildings in your area. Oftentimes, jewelers will go in on studio spaces together so they can share tools and expensive equipment. This could be great if you are first starting out and don't have much equipment of your own yet. If you're looking for a shared space to set up your studio, reach out to your local school, college, or other artists to see if they know of anything available.

You can rent bench space hourly, daily, or even permanently from many jewelry schools. Oftentimes, this comes with the use of equipment, and sometimes a studio monitor to help answer any questions you have.

If you specialize in design and use outside contractors to produce your jewelry, look for a coworking space where you can rent a desk. There are tons of coworking spaces popping up all over the place and you may enjoy the shared energy of other entrepreneurs. Coworking spaces often include shared office supplies, kitchens, conference rooms, and other amenities you may find attractive.

Private Artist's Studio

Rent your own private studio if you need the space and enjoy the privacy. Look for a small commercial space in an industrial area or an already established artists' building. This will be ideal if you have the tools and equipment you need to set up a studio, and if your company grows to bring in other employees to work in your space. Make sure your space is secure, especially if you are working late and have expensive materials and equipment on hand. Go with your gut: if you have a bad feeling about an area or a space, look for someplace else.

ESSENTIAL STUDIO TOOLS AND EQUIPMENT

Hand Tools

Even if you don't plan to physically produce your jewelry, it is crucial to understand the basics of jewelry making. Knowing what it takes to create a piece of jewelry will make you a better designer and will help you when you're working with contractors and employees. By grasping all aspects of your business, you will excel at sales and marketing, too. Here is a list of hand tools most jewelers use.

JEWELER'S SAW FRAME

This is an important and versatile tool in the jewelry studio. Purchase a 4-inch- (10-cm) deep saw frame to use as a multipurpose tool; you may need a 6-inch- (15-cm) deep frame for cutting larger pieces of material. Load your saw frame with metal saw blades to cut out shapes in metal and wire, and cut off sprues from castings. Load your saw frame with a spiral wax blade to cut out shapes in wax blanks.

METAL SAW BLADES

Sold by the dozen, these paper-thin blades are great for cutting through metal, but they break easily. Find the proper saw blade for the metal you are cutting to avoid breaking more blades than necessary and to minimize your frustration while cutting. Purchase your blades by the gross, or twelve dozen (144), to always have them on hand and receive a price break. If you are cutting shapes out of 20-gauge metal, about 1 millimeter thick, use a #1 blade. If you are cutting the sprue off a casting, use a #1 blade. Use the chart on this page to help find the correct blade size. There are many expensive versions of saw blades whose manufacturers claim they are unbreakable. I recommend not spending more money than you need to on saw blades, since you will probably be stocking up on them pretty regularly.

SPIRAL WAX SAW BLADES

Manufactured specifically for cutting through wax, these blades are used in a jeweler's saw frame to cut through wax quickly. When loading the blade into the jeweler's saw frame, there is no top

METAL SAW BLADE CHART

Blade Size	Blade Thickness	Blade Depth	Teeth per Inch	Metal Gauge Recommendation	Drill Bit Size
8/0	.0063"	.0126"	89.0	up to 26	80
7/0	.0067"	.0130"	84.0	24–26	80
6/0	.0070"	.0140"	76.0	24	79
5/0	.0080"	.0157"	71.0	22–24	78
4/0	.0086"	.0175"	66.0	22	76
3/0	.0095"	.0190"	61.0	22	76
2/0	.0103"	.0204"	56.0	20–22	75
*1/0	.0110"	.0220"	53.5	18–22	73
1	.0120"	.0240"	51.0	18–20	71
2	.0134"	.0276"	43.0	16–18	70
3	.0140"	.0290"	40.5	16–18	68
4	.0150"	.0307"	38.0	16–18	67
5	.0158"	.0331"	35.5	16	65
6	.0173"	.0370"	33.0	14	58
7	.0189"	.0400"	30.5	12	57
8	.0197"	.0440"	28.0	12	55

*most commonly used sawblade

or bottom of the blade. Start your cut by drawing your saw blade up to help mark your spot, then cut straight up and down at a 90-degree angle. To create a more intricate pattern, try using a metal saw blade.

When you load your saw frame, insert the blade facing out, with the teeth facing down into the loosened wing nut closest to the handle. Saw frames are somewhat flexible. While pushing the top of your saw frame against your bench, insert the far end of the saw blade into the top wing nut and tighten. When you pluck the saw blade, it should sound like a note on a musical instrument and feel taut. If it sounds flat, unscrew the top wing nut and try again to make it taut.

METAL FILES

These are essentials on every jeweler's bench. Start with a half-round hand file, which is extremely versatile for filing flat and convex shapes with the flat side, and concave shapes, like the inside of a ring, with the round side. Also invest in an inexpensive set of needle files, which generally come in a pack of six 6-inch- (15-cm) long files. Purchase cut #0, which are coarse files that will shape and soften metal quickly.

DOUBLE-ENDED WAX FILE

This file is ideal for the beginning stages of carving a shape because it removes material quickly. Use the coarse side to create a rough shape, and then switch to the fine side to begin to refine. This file is too coarse to use on metal, so be sure to use it only on wax.

You can use the same set of needle files on wax and metal, but invest in a file-cleaning brush to clean your files before switching between materials so you don't cross contaminate.

CUTTING TEETH

Like all other tools, files have their own system of grading how coarse or fine they are, called a cut. The most versatile cuts are #0 files, which are coarse.

#00: extremely coarse, for removing a lot of material

#0: coarse, for removing material and shaping; all-purpose file

#2: medium coarseness, for shaping and smoothing

#4: fine coarseness, for shaping and smoothing

#6: extra-fine coarseness, for shaping and smoothing

SHAPES

Metal files come in many different shapes and sizes to help shape and smooth your materials. If you are filing a flat or convex

area, use a flat file. If you are filing a concave area, use a half-round or round file. For shaping materials, always match the file to the shape you are trying to make. For example, if you are filing a sharp V-shape in your metal, use a triangle-shaped file.

Metal files come in shapes like flat, half-round, round, square, triangle, and barrette. Barrette files are extremely handy because they have teeth only on the bottom, not on their sides or on top. These are great when you are trying to avoid filing an area that is next to where you are filing. Use masking tape to block off an area to avoid filing it.

FILE CARE

Steel tools rust when they are exposed to water. So make sure you dry your jewelry pieces after they get wet to avoid getting your steel tools wet. Every so often, use a rag to wipe your steel tools down with an all-purpose tool oil. Store your tools in a cool, dry place. If your steel tools rust, use a coarse sandpaper to remove the rust and then wipe down with an all-purpose oil. Plastic and wood file holders are available to make using your files more comfortable. I like to use a champagne cork as my file holder; I find it ergonomic and more comfortable for my small hands. Plus, champagne corks are free after you drink a bottle.

PLIERS

Pliers are a hand tool used to manipulate sheet metal and wire. The most common pliers are flat-nose, round-nose, and half-round pliers. Use flat-nose pliers to grip metal so it doesn't slip, and to manipulate it, as when you swing open a jump ring. Use round-nose pliers to curve the metal by guiding it with the round shape, as when you make a hook on the end of an earring wire. Use half-round pliers to form rings or other round shapes by putting the round part in the inside, and the flat part on the outside. Don't waste your money buying fancy pliers; the inexpensive ones work great and you can replace them when needed.

DENTAL AND CARVING TOOLS

Use these to create textures in your wax, take away material, and refine your design. You can get a very inexpensive set of dental tools in a variety of shapes at a hardware store or online. Instead of investing in an expensive set of carving tools, sharpen your dental tools on a sharpening stone, with an old metal file, or on a grinding wheel. A dental tool with a sharp edge will carve away material fast.

Yes, these are the same tools that dentists use! In fact, many tools are very similar in the dental and jewelry industry. I have met quite a few dentists who have dabbled in jewelry making.

METAL DIVIDER AND RULER

A divider is probably the most widely used tool for jewelry making. Use your divider to mark measurements on your metal and wax for height, width, length, and decorative elements. Use a ruler with a metric side to measure everything out in millimeters.

SANDPAPER AND ABRASIVES

EMERY PAPER

This is a type of sandpaper that is very coarse and used to smooth out rough surfaces. It is great for softening sharp pieces and getting out really deep scratches.

WET/DRY SANDPAPER

Purchase sheets of wet/dry sandpaper through a jewelry-supply store or even your local hardware store. To finish your pieces, use coarse sandpaper to fine sandpaper to soften and get out all the scratches. The lower the number, the coarser the paper. The most common grits are 220 (coarse), 320 (medium), 400 (fine), and 600 (extra fine). You will often see these four grits sold in a packet together.

Move the flat side of your jewelry piece in small circles and figure eights on top of your sandpaper on a flat surface to flat-sand your piece. Wrap your sandpaper around a file, or adhere it around a popsicle stick or a paint stirrer, to make sanding sticks. Cut a strip and wrap it around a metal bur, which you then insert into a flex shaft to sand, shape, and cut your material.

Polishing Cloth

This is a staple in every jewelry studio. Purchase a polishing cloth, which is a rag that is infused with a polishing compound. A polishing compound has a very fine grit, which burnishes the metal surface so finely that it shines.

ESSENTIAL MACHINES

Anything you can do by hand, you can do faster by machine. To speed up production in your studio, consider investing in some machines to do things more efficiently.

When working with machines, make sure you know how to safely operate them. Always pay attention to what you are doing and what's in front of you. When you're distracted and moving too fast, you tend to get hurt. Always wear safety goggles when operating machinery. To avoid getting something caught in a rotary tool, tie long hair back and don't wear any loose-fitting

clothing when operating the machine. All machines need proper upkeep to prolong their useful life. Ask the manufacturer about proper care and cleaning, and for any specific safety instructions.

Flexible Shaft

This is the most versatile machine in the studio. The flexible shaft, or flex shaft, is a rotary tool with a long, flexible hose and a hand piece. A bur is a thin steel attachment that gets inserted into the flex shaft. There are hundreds of burs available for many different purposes: drilling, sanding, grinding, texturing, and more. Hold your hand piece straight up at a 90-degree angle, and insert your bur into the collette, or teeth, that will hold your bur in. Place your bur in straight and make sure that all three teeth are holding the bur equally. Tighten the collette using the key attachment. Press on the pedal lightly so the collette and the bur rotate. This versatile machine can be used for cutting, grinding, sanding, polishing, cutting seats for stone settings, and texturing.

ESSENTIAL BURS

Assorted Drill Bits: Available in various sizes, these are used for drilling holes in metal and other materials to attach jump rings and rivets, or to prep seats for stone setting.

Sanding Burs: There are countless types of burs available to soften, shape, and sand scratches out of your pieces.

A split mandrel is a cylinder-shaped steel bur with a split down the center. Insert a strip of sandpaper the same width as the opening, and when you run the flex shaft it will rotate to sand your piece. This is a great way to quickly change your sandpaper grit without changing your bur.

A screw mandrel is a cylinder-shaped steel bur with a small screw that screws into the top. The screw holds in attachments, like silicone wheels, which help shape and soften pieces. Cut a 1-inch (2.5-cm) circle out of your sandpaper, drill a hole in the center, and secure it into the bur with the screw. This is a wonderful custom sanding bur and works well getting into small crevices.

A rubber barrel is a steel bur with a rubber cylinder attached to the end, usually around ¼ inch (6 mm) in diameter. You can purchase sanding barrels to insert onto the cylinder, or create your own by wrapping a strip of sandpaper tightly around the barrel and securing it with some super-strong glue. This creates a sharp edge of sandpaper, which is perfect for getting into small corners.

There are many types of grinding burs that you can use in a lot of different ways. Cylinder and ball burs are metal burs used to grind down large chunks of metal or wax, create textures, and cut seats for setting gemstones. Diamond-coated burs work well to grind and shape metal. They come in various shapes and are coated with finely ground, tool-grade diamonds that cut very quickly. Some flex shafts come with a variety of burs in a kit; test them out and purchase other types and shapes as needed.

Use polishing burs to shine your pieces using a flex shaft. Use a felt or muslin wheel with a polishing compound to polish your piece. In a pinch, cut a cotton swab in half and insert it into your flex shaft with some polishing compound (page 64). This is certainly effective, but cotton swabs will wear out quickly.

Wax Injector

A wax injector is a pressurized machine that heats up wax so it can be injected into a two-part mold. It's available with a hand pump or an air compressor to pressurize the machine. Lightly brush the inside of your two-part mold with talcum powder or mold release spray to help avoid breaking the wax as you take it out of the mold. Find an injection wax that you like working with and fill the chamber up about 80 percent full. Heat the wax between 155°F and 160°F (68–71°C), or as the manufacturer suggests, and press the opening of your mold into the nozzle as the wax shoots out for about five seconds. Wax injectors are very helpful if you do a lot of model making in wax and lost-wax casting.

Rolling Mill

Traditionally, this is used for making metal sheet by compressing the piece of metal through two steel cylinders and making the sheet thinner and longer. Keep sending your metal through the rolling mill until you have reached the desired thickness. Keep your metal pliable so it doesn't crack by annealing it (page 67) every time you take a pass through the rolling mill. You can also use a mill to texturize your metal. Sandwich your metal with another material, like a piece of lace or tree bark, and put it through the rolling mill. The texture will be embossed on the metal. Your material may get ruined by being passed through the rolling mill, so don't use anything too precious.

Polishing Wheel

A muslin or felt wheel is put on the rotary machine and lightly coated with a polishing compound to finish the piece. Polishing compound is a claylike substance with very fine grit mixed in to polish the surface of the metal and make it shiny. The felt or muslin wheel doesn't do the polishing; the compound does. If you have more than one type of compound, don't mix up the wheels and burs you use them on to avoid cross contamination. First use a cutting compound, or what is sometimes referred to as *prepolish*. This compound is mixed with grit to use as a final stage, or finishing, and get out all the scratches. After washing off the excess compound with warm, soapy water and a soft brush or in an ultrasonic machine (page 66), use the polishing wheel to put a final finish on your piece, if desired. You can use a high-luster polishing compound, like rouge, for a high-polished finish. You can also use a matte wheel or a brush wheel for a more subtle finish on your metal.

Rotary Tumbler

A rotary tumbler is a great machine for both small- and large-scale production. Instead of polishing each piece by hand, or on the polishing wheel, use a tumbler to batch-polish your pieces. A tumbler is a rotating barrel filled with water; small stainless steel, ceramic, or plastic bits in different shapes called shot; and a compound that polishes your pieces. A tumbler can burnish your metal to look shiny, work harden it (page 68), and remove any excess residue on the piece. Once your jewelry pieces are completely finished and ready for polishing, place them in the tumbler for at least four hours. I like to leave my tumbler going overnight so my pieces are polished and any sharp areas become softened. Don't place any softer, porous stones, like opal or turquoise, in the tumbler, but harder stones, such as diamonds, rubies, and sapphires, should be fine. Always test one piece for twenty minutes and then check it if you are not sure how well it will do in the tumbler.

For a high-shine finish, use stainless-steel shot, and for a matte finish, use plastic shot. You can buy burnishing solutions to mix with water in your tumbler. I prefer using a small squirt of natural dishwashing soap mixed with half steel shot and half plastic shot for a semi shiny finish.

For large-scale production, you can use an abrasive medium to debur and sand your pieces. Factory production is done in this manner by tumbling batches with coarse to fine abrasive media. Purchase multiple tumblers, designating each one for a specific grit, and cycle pieces in the tumbler for a few hours in each. I wouldn't recommend this method for pieces with a lot of detail. You will start to lose some quality and handmade details with this method.

If your tumbler becomes dirty, make sure to clean it really well so the dirt doesn't contaminate any of your pieces. Rinse your barrel out well after each use and do not store your shot in the barrel or in water. Periodically run a twenty-minute cleansing cycle of 50 percent water and 50 percent distilled white vinegar, and then rinse, followed by twenty minutes with enough water to cover your shot and 1 tablespoon (15 ml) of baking soda. If you use your tumbler daily, consider doing a rinse cycle once a week.

Ultrasonic Machine

Used to clean metal and jewelry, an ultrasonic machine has a heated water bath with a cleaning solution that vibrates at ultrasonic frequencies. Ultrasonic frequencies are sounds that are higher-pitched than humans can hear. This loosens any compound or dirt in the jewelry and leaves it pristine. An ultrasonic machine is great to use in between polishing compounds to fully clean the piece.

Steam Cleaner

Using pressurized steam from regular tap water, a steam cleaner loosens dirt and cleans jewelry and gemstones. This is a terrific tool to use after polishing or to brighten jewelry after it has been worn for a while.

BASIC JEWELRY-MAKING TECHNIQUES

Whether you have been studying jewelry for fifty years or you are just beginning, it is vital to know about the basic techniques of jewelry fabrication. Even if you are not a master, having a foundation of basic techniques, tools, and industry processes will yield better designs and well-made jewelry. When designing a production line, it's important to create a master piece, sometimes referred to as your *model*, to represent the exact look, feel, and finish of what the production pieces will look like. You can create your model using a variety of jewelry techniques including metal fabrication, wax carving, and computer-aided design (CAD).

Metal-Fabrication

Metal fabrication refers to the process of manipulating wire and sheet metal by cutting, bending, and shaping the metal to construct a piece of jewelry or another object.

CUTTING AND PIERCING

Simple or intricate patterns can be cut into your piece by using a jeweler's saw frame and a metal saw blade. Cut out a paper pattern and adhere it to your sheet metal with rubber cement, then draw directly onto your metal with a sharpie or scratch in lines with a sharp scribe. Use your saw frame to cut straight up and down at a 90-degree angle with your dominant hand. Steer the metal with your nondominant hand to follow the pattern you are cutting. Think of your saw frame as a scroll saw, moving up and down in a stationary position. Guide the metal with your nondominant hand. Especially if you're a beginner, cut on the outside of your line so you can file your pattern smooth if you make any mistakes. To cut out an area on the inside of the metal, drill a hole and thread your saw blade through it.

BENDING AND FORMING

Start with a flat sheet of metal or wire, and anneal it to become soft and malleable. Once it is annealed, form your metal around a ring or bracelet mandrel or another shape. Depending on the thickness of your metal, use the force of your fingers as much as you can to manipulate it. When you can't use your hands anymore, hammer your piece into shape. Use a plastic or raw hide hammer to keep the current texture on your metal, and use a metal hammer to add hammer marks while shaping.

Put sharp bends into your piece by scoring your metal with a triangle or square file up to halfway through the thickness of your piece, depending on the angle you are trying to achieve. Use flat-nose pliers to bend the metal and create the angle you are looking to achieve. Solder the bend shut to stabilize your piece.

CARVING AND FILING

Use metal files to soften the edges of your metal after cutting and to change the shape of your piece. When filing, put your force into your stroke as the file goes forward to use it most effectively. The teeth are manufactured so you file away from yourself, as opposed to filing toward yourself, since you have more strength while pushing. File the edges so your lines look clean and flat, and at a 45-degree angle to make your piece very soft. Use a diamond bur on the flex shaft to carve and create shape in your metal.

ANNEALING

To soften your metal, gently heat the whole piece evenly by using a flame from a torch (page 70). Place your metal on a charcoal block or solderite board, which can withstand the heat. By heating the metal, you are altering the physical structure of the metal to make it more malleable and softer to work with. Essentially, you are making space in between the molecules to allow for movement. When annealing, aim to heat your metal evenly, as if it were in an oven, by moving your flame consistently around the whole piece. Once you see the first sign of a slight glow, your piece is annealed. Let the metal air-cool for a few minutes and then quench it in water using steel tweezers with a wooden handle. Now your metal will be more malleable to form into shapes by using hammers around ring and bracelet mandrels or by using metal pliers. As you hammer your metal and use steel tools, you are pushing those molecules back together, a process called work hardening. When your metal feels like the resistance is back and it's springy, anneal again if needed. Once your metal is fully formed, make sure to purposely work harden it by using a hammer on a steel block or a mandrel, or by placing it in a rotary tumbler. If you don't work harden your piece, it will slowly lose its shape over time and not function properly as a wearable piece of jewelry

SOLDERING AND PICKLING

Soldering refers to joining two or more metals by melting a filler metal that has a lower melting temperature into the joint. Soldering can be simple if you keep in mind these few key pointers: Make sure all your metal is really clean. Make sure the seam where you intend to solder the pieces together is straight and doesn't have any gaps. Heat your metal evenly.

Set your piece up to solder so the joints are touching seamlessly on a charcoal or solderite board. If you need to, set up your piece by using cross-lock tweezers in a third arm to hold it in place. Paint a small amount of flux—a chemical used to keep your metal from oxidizing while it heats up—on your solder seam. Place a piece of solder in the seam. Using a flame from a torch, heat your piece evenly, as if it were in an oven. Once you see it anneal—that is, when you see the first sign of a gentle glow—move your flame back and forth

on the seam, and you will see your solder ball up and then flow into the seam and the solder will resemble mercury. Let your piece air-cool for a few minutes, quench it in water, and place it in the pickle (see page 69) for a few minutes to clean. After your solder is complete and your piece is pickled, file the excess solder away and make sure the seam isn't visible.

TYPES OF SOLDER

Solder is a low-melting alloy used to join two pieces of metal together. For jewelry, solder is available for all alloys and colors of gold, platinum, silver, and brass. Solder comes in different melting temperatures and is available in hard, medium, and easy. For silver solder, hard solder has the highest melting temperature and also contains the most silver. Medium has a slightly lower melting point because it has a little less silver and a little more tin, and so on with easy solder. Begin by using hard solder; you may choose to use medium solder for your next seam so it doesn't open. To prevent a solder seam from flowing again, mix yellow ochre with water to create a thin paint and paint it on the seam. In a pinch you can use white correction fluid, but I highly recommend wearing a mask while heating that up. You can

purchase solder in many forms including sheet, wire, prechopped chips, and paste.

PICKLE

Pickle is a solution used to clean a piece after it is soldered. For this purpose, you can use store-bought granular acid that you dissolve in water, and heat it in a small slow cooker when in use. Pickle cleans away the firescale—a layer of oxides brought to the surface when heated in the soldering process—by eating away at the outside layer of the piece. Don't put steel in your pickle solution; that prompts a chemical reaction that plates the outside of your pieces with copper and will be frustrating to clean. Instead, use copper- or plastic-coated tweezers, which don't generate a chemical reaction, to get your piece out of the pickle and then dunk it in water to get the excess pickle solution off. If you get some of the pickle solution on your body or clothes, rub it with baking soda to neutralize the solution. When using the granular acid, make sure to check the manufacturer's MSDS, or material safety data sheet, for information on how to use and dispose of it.

For a natural solution, use a solution of 2 cups (475 ml) distilled white vinegar and

¼ cup (60 ml) of table salt, hence the name *pickle*. Heat the vinegar up in the slow cooker and dissolve the table salt right in it. To dispose of this, dilute it with water and pour it down the drain. This solution works great but will have to be changed more than the store-bought solution.

TYPES OF GAS AND TORCH SYSTEMS

There are many different gases to use for a soldering station setup. Compressed acetylene, propane, oxygen-acetylene, and natural gases are all commonly used to solder jewelry. Purchase a tank with a hose, regulator, and torch handle at a local gas-supply store. Torch tips are interchangeable and come in many sizes, so I recommend starting out with a small- and a medium-size one at first. Depending on where you live and where your studio is set up, you may need a license to operate a torch. Certain types of gas tanks are not allowed in residential buildings, so be sure to check with your local municipality. Secure your gas tank to the wall or table with a chain or a bungee cord. If you own and operate a gas tank, you should know how to change and empty the tank out, check for leaks, and care for it. If you suspect a leak, mix together a solution of a squirt of dish soap and half a cup of water. Coat the solution on the valve of your tank, the hose, and your torch handle. Turn on your tank, and if you see bubbles, you have a leak. If you notice a leak, turn your tank off immediately and drain the hose. Wrap a single layer of thread seal tape (Teflon tape) to patch up the leak. Retest with soapy water. If your leak is still there, you may need to replace a part and call your local gas supply store. Turn your tank off at the end of the day when you leave your studio, drain the hose, and release the pressure.

For small solders, many jewelers use a micro torch filled with butane, or the small torch a pastry chef uses for crème brûlée. They are really handy to have around and can solder small jump rings and thin wire rings.

Make sure you have good ventilation by your torch setup. You can install a hood vent over your soldering station that draws the fumes outside. You should at least have a window open with a ventilation fan pulling air outside.

SURFACE PATTERN TECHNIQUES

There are many different options to add decorative elements to your piece. Make sure your patterns and colors are consistent and that anything you add to your pieces won't come off. Perform many tests for your techniques before you add them to a production line to make sure you have worked out all the kinks.

Oxidation and Patina

An amazing way to bring out the details of your work is oxidizing your metal or adding a patina to make it look like an antique. Use a solution like liver of sulfur on sterling silver, copper, and bronze to add a blackened finish to your piece. Lightly sand or polish to highlight the pattern on the surface, so the black stays in the recessed areas. Read the package for information on how to mix and store your liver of sulfur. To dispose of it, dilute it in water and pour it down the drain. Premixed patinas in many colors are also available for metal. Check the MSDS, or material safety data sheet, on how to dispose of these. Patinas can be applied to metal jewelry that is fabricated and cast.

Reticulation

Reticulation is a surface pattern technique that occurs on sterling silver just before it reaches its melting temperature. Sterling silver is made up of copper and fine silver, which have slightly different melting

temperatures. This disparity creates buckles, wrinkles, and cracks in the metal as it begins to melt. Heat the piece evenly and you will see the metal start to buckle, move, and shrink to create an intricate pattern. This happens very quickly, so use a small torch tip and pay attention.

Enamel

Enamel is created by powdered glass that is sifted over metals like copper, silver, and gold and heated up in a kiln or with a torch. The glass melts and solidifies onto the piece. There are many beautiful and intricate ancient techniques for applying enamel. You can achieve different surface patterns by controlling the firing time and layering different colors of enamel in between firings. There's also low-fire enamel paint, which can be painted onto the metal and cured at a much lower temperature. This material is often used on base metals like brass and bronze. In general, enameling is one of the last steps in creating a piece of jewelry. Enamel can be applied to jewelry that is fabricated and cast.

Resin

Resin refers to many different materials that start as a liquid and set with a hard, plastic-like finish. Liquid resin can be poured into molds and mixed with color, paper, dried plants, and other objects, and cured to harden. You can also pour metal directly onto your piece in a concave surface.

Keum-Boo

This is an ancient Korean technique of attaching pure gold foil to other pure metals like fine silver and copper. It is a beautiful process and a great way to add gold to jewelry inexpensively. Your metal is heated up to around 550°F (288°C), and the gold foil is burnished on top, attaching to the metal by a diffusion bond. This process can be done in an open kiln, with a torch, or with a hot plate. I prefer to use a hot plate for this technique with a piece of 16-gauge

brass sheet on the plate to spread the heat evenly. Place your clean metal on the brass plate, and when the piece reaches optimal temperature, use a steel or agate burnisher to apply pressure to the gold foil to bond them together. Keum-boo can be applied to jewelry that is fabricated and cast. To apply keum-boo to sterling silver, it must be depletion guided first. Anneal your sterling silver five to seven times, placing it in the pickle each time to bring the fine silver to the surface. This will allow the pure gold to bond to the pure silver on the surface.

STONE SETTING

A great way to add color and sparkle to your jewelry is to incorporate gemstones.

Approach setting your stones as a matter of problem solving and figure out the best way to feature the stone in your design securely with a matching aesthetic. Learn to build settings and set gemstones yourself, purchase premade settings to use in your work, or contract the work out to a professional stone setter.

Bezel Setting

This is the most basic setting. A thin wall of metal surrounds the stone to hold it in place. Bezel settings protect the stone, especially if it is fragile, and have less chances of snagging clothing or getting caught on things. Fabricate your bezel settings in metal or build them in wax.

Prong Setting

This claw-shaped setting typically has three, four, or six prongs to hold the stone in place. It's a beautiful setting for featuring a gemstone without covering up too much of the stone. Keep in mind that if prongs aren't finished correctly, they can be sharp and snag on clothing. Use a cup bur in your flex shaft, the same diameter as your prongs, to round out the edges without affecting your stone. Fabricate your prong settings in metal or build them in wax. A cup bur has teeth on the inside to grind the edge of the prong to become

round and soft without affecting the surface of the stone, so it's the perfect tool.

FLUSH, GYPSY, OR SURFACE SETTING

Set tiny stones into the metal's surface by drilling a hole, or seat, for the stone so it fits in flush with the metal. This is called flush, gypsy, or surface setting. Push a little metal over the stone to hold it in place by using a burnishing tool. This is a popular setting because it can be simple, has a minimalist look, and adds some sparkle.

Pavé Setting

Pavé setting refers to placing an array of faceted gemstones right next to one another so you can barely see the metal underneath. The stones are held in place by tiny prongs or beads pushed over the stones.

Channel Setting

In this type of setting, gemstones are held together in a row by two strips of metal on either side, with no additional prongs or beads.

WHERE TO PURCHASE GEMSTONES

Gemstones are pieces of mineral crystals that can be left raw or cut and polished to make jewelry. Some organic materials that are not minerals are also used in jewelry and considered gemstones, like lapis lazuli and jet. Gemstones are measured in hardness by the Mohs hardness scale. Diamonds are the hardest natural gemstone at a 10, and talc is the softest at 1. When choosing gemstones to set, aim to select harder stones—those that are a 7 or above—to avoid having the stones crack or crumble when the customers wear them. If you're working with softer stones, like turquoise or opal, make sure the settings are secure and the stones aren't too exposed to avoiding cracking. Gemstones vary greatly in price, depending on their rarity and hardness. Synthetic gemstones are widely available today and are generally less expensive than natural ones and are free from inclusions and blemishes.

MOHS HARDNESS SCALE FOR THE FIFTY MOST POPULAR GEMS

10: Diamond

9.5: Moissanite

9: Corundum, Cubic Zirconia, Ruby, Sapphire

8–9: Alexandrite

8: Aquamarine, Chrysoberyl, Emerald, Spinel, Topaz

7–7.5: Iolite

7: Agate, Amethyst, Ametrine, Ammonite, Aventurine, Carnelian, Chalcedony, Citrine, Garnet, Jasper, Onyx, Peridot, Quartz, Sardonyx, Tiger's Eye, Tourmaline, Zircon

6.5–7: Tanzanite

6: Chrysocolla, Chrysoprase, Hematite, Jade, Labradorite, Lapis Lazuli, Moonstone, Opal, Sodalite, Turquoise

5.5–6: Chrome Diopside

4: Jet, Rhodochrosite

3.5–4: Malachite

3: Coral, Pearl

2–6: Serpentine

2: Amber, Ivory

Source: Tim McCreight, The Complete Metalsmith

Gemstones can be purchased online from gemstone companies, in person at a gem company store, or from a representative who works directly with the mine. You can even find gemstones at some retail stores and outdoor markets. For jewelry production, look into buying a batch of calibrated gemstones that are all the same size. If you can't find what you're looking for, you can get stones custom cut in any shape and size from a lapidary.

TYPES OF METAL AND WHERE TO PURCHASE THEM

A pure metal, or element, is found in nature and consists of one type of molecule, while an alloy is human-made by mixing two or more metals to come up with a mixture. Examples of metals used in jewelry are gold, platinum, palladium, silver, and copper. Metals like pure gold and silver are very beautiful but extremely malleable, and too soft to use in creating jewelry. Mixtures of different metals create alloys that are stronger and can be hardened to hold their shape for making jewelry. Examples of alloys used in jewelry are all karats and colors of gold, sterling silver, brass, and bronze.

Fine Metals and Alloys

Other metals are added to pure, or fine, gold to achieve different colors and increase toughness and hardness. The word *karat* refers to a unit of measure indicating how pure the gold is. In other words, karat refers to how many parts of gold are in the mixture (see chart below). The word comes

24K	or	100	refers to	100% pure gold content
22K	or	916	refers to	91.6% pure gold content
18K	or	750	refers to	75% pure gold content
14K	or	585	refers to	58.5% pure gold content
10K	or	416	refers to	41.6% pure gold content

from the carob seed, which was used as a measure at ancient markets throughout Asia. In most countries, laws require fine metals to be stamped to indicate their purity. You may notice a piece of jewelry with "14K" or the number "585" stamped on it. This refers to the pure gold content.

Sterling silver is a mixture, or alloy, of 92.5 percent fine silver and 7.5 percent copper (or other metal), sometimes marked as 925, or sterling. Fine silver, a metal found in nature, is very soft and not able to be hardened to hold a shape. Fine silver is often used in jewelry to make earrings or bezel wire, or enhanced with enamel, because the malleability does not play a factor. Traditionally, copper is added to silver to create sterling silver, which can be hardened and hold its shape. This also results in oxidation because of the copper.

Sterling silver can be purchased hard (or prehardened) or soft (or preannealed). There is generally no price difference between the two.

Base Metals and Alloys

Base metals are metals or alloys that don't have any fine metals in their composition. Examples of base metals used in the jewelry industry are copper, brass, and bronze. Oftentimes, base metals are plated with a thin coat of fine metal. More and more jewelry designers are leaving brass and bronze unplated in their designs as the price of fine metals continues to rise. Brass is an alloy of copper and zinc, and bronze is an alloy of mostly copper and tin. Nickel is sometimes added to brass and bronze and is a common allergen, so be sure to check with your sources about whether there is any nickel in the brass or bronze you're purchasing.

Metal Forms

Hundreds, even thousands of years ago, metalsmiths would create their own metal alloys by melting metals together in a crucible and pouring them into a steel frame, or ingot mold. They would then make metal sheet by rolling it through a rolling mill, or make metal wire by pulling the metal through a steel plate with holes of varying diameter to draw the metal down to the correct size. In our modern world, metal can be purchased in many different premade forms. You can purchase sheet, wire, and premade chains and findings from online or brick-and-mortar metal-supply stores.

Sheet Metal

Sheet metal, like all fine and base metals, is available in a variety of thicknesses, or gauges. The lower the gauge number, the thicker the metal. An 18-gauge sheet, which is about 1 millimeter thick, is a good all-purpose thickness for sheet metal. This is ideal for sawing out shapes for pendants, rings, and earrings. To make a cuff bracelet, use a thicker gauge, like 14-gauge. Sheet metal is also available with embossed textures and surface patterns.

Wire

Wire in all fine and base metals is available in a variety of thicknesses, or gauges, and shapes. You can purchase round, half-round, square, and triangle-shaped wire. You can also purchase patterned wire, which is great for making bezel settings for gemstones. A 12-gauge wire is ideal for a simple bangle. A 16-gauge wire works well for a simple wire ring. A 22-gauge wire is ideal for earring wires and posts.

WAX CARVING TECHNIQUES

Carving wax is a material you can shape to make three-dimensional models to be cast into metal. The subtractive technique involves taking material away using files, carving tools, and burs to reveal a design. The additive technique involves adding wax by melting it, placing it, and shaping it to build up a surface or decorative elements. Once you have created your wax

model, you can then cast the piece into metal using the lost-wax casting technique (page 81). You can use the same tools and techniques to finish and polish cast pieces as you would finish your jewelry that you fabricated.

Types of Wax and Choosing the Right Material

SOFT WAX

Soft and pliable sheet wax is available in pink (soft) and green (semisoft). It's ideal for making bezels and adding decorative accents to a piece. Soft sheet wax is very difficult to clean and can be scratched easily, so be sure to add decorative elements with soft wax as the last step. This kind of wax will get more pliable as you manipulate it; it warms up if in contact with your body or if it's hot out. Put it in the fridge for a few minutes to make it harden if you are having trouble working with it.

HARD WAX

Ideal for carving shapes using the subtractive technique, hard wax almost feels like plastic with nice resistance. It is available in a variety of hardnesses. The following information is always available on the outside of a package when you purchase wax, so don't worry if you can't commit it to memory. Hard carving wax comes in a variety of forms. Pick the right form, or blank, depending on what you are designing.

Green: The most rigid wax. Ideal for carving intricate details, and it holds textures really well.

Purple: A great all-purpose wax with medium flexibility. Works well for most projects.

Blue: The most flexible hard wax. Best for carving pieces with no texture. It has some bend to it.

Injection Wax: Used in a wax injection machine to inject hot, liquid wax into a silicone or rubber mold to make multiples. This comes in a variety of hardnesses but is generally harder and more brittle than carving wax.

Basic Wax Carving Techniques

MEASURING AND CUTTING

Using your divider, scroll out the arms on your ruler to transfer the measurement onto your piece of wax. Depending on your design, measure the height, width, length, and any other dimensions you need. A divider is very handy, since it locks the measurement in place without moving. If you are having trouble using your divider on wax, try holding it like a pencil and drawing with a lighter touch, so the sharp arms don't get stuck in the wax. Use your spiral wax blade, tightened in your jeweler's saw frame. Start by running your blade up to help get the blade to cut straight on the line. With your saw frame, cut straight up and down at a 90-degree angle.

SIZING A RING

Start with a wax blank with a premade hole. Use your wax ring mandrel and insert it into the ring blank. Make a few full turns, and flip the ring so you can insert the ring mandrel from the other side. Check the ring size on a metal ring mandrel. When it's cast in metal, the ring will shrink a little, but it will get a little larger as you clean and sand the inside. Carve your ring to the exact size you are aiming for.

CREATING AN OVERALL SHAPE

Use your files to create the overall shape of your piece. To remove material faster, use a grinding bur, like a ball or a cylinder bur, in your flex shaft. Treat this as if you were sketching and just trying to get the overall shape. You can add details later.

TEXTURING

Now that you have the overall shape, add details using needle files and carving tools. You can use a wide variety of burs to create texture in your pieces. You can achieve just about any texture in wax or just make a smooth and clean finish.

ADDITIVE TECHNIQUE

Build up an area of your piece or insert decorative elements by adding wax using dental tools and an alcohol lamp, a battery-operated wax pen, or an electric wax pen. You can use relief wax to build up an area and then carve details into it, or add decorative elements like granules. Use heat to repair a crack in your wax or attach two or more pieces together.

FINISHING AND PREPPING YOUR PIECE FOR CASTING

When carving wax, you should get in the habit of using sandpaper or other tools to remove all scratches. You want to do as much work in the wax as possible so your model, or metal casting, comes out with very little cleanup. Use wet/dry sandpaper, from coarse to fine, to remove scratches. Use a sanding stick or wrap your sandpaper around the same file you use to carve the wax. If you have a lot of texture, you may want to skip the coarse sandpaper and go directly to the fine. You can also use a felt wheel, extra-fine steel wool, and a polishing cloth to take out more scratches. Try them all and see what works best for you and your designs (read about the casting process on page 81).

HOW TO CLEAN A CASTING

Once your model is cast from wax to metal, the first step is to remove the sprue. Using your jeweler's saw frame and a metal saw blade, cut off the sprue. Hold your saw frame up 90 degrees and cut straight through without making a sharp turn or your blade will snap. Save your sprues in a bag, and bring them back to your caster to receive a credit or send them to be refined with the rest of your scrap. Now that the sprue is cut off, file the remainder of the sprue all the way down so you can't see it anymore. For a faster option, use a metal grinding bur or a rubber barrel with 80-grit sandpaper to remove the excess metal. Now finish the casting with the same sanding and polishing techniques you would with fabricated jewelry.

SANDING

Once you have shaped and formed your piece of fabricated jewelry or de-sprued your metal casting, the final steps are finishing your piece. Remove all the scratches and make your metal feel soft by sanding your piece with coarse- to fine-grit sandpaper. Not every piece is finished in the same way. If you have a piece with lots of texture, consider skipping the coarsest sandpaper and going straight to the fine. If you are sanding by hand, go down to a 600-grit sandpaper. If you are sanding on a machine, 400-grit sandpaper should do the trick.

FINISHING AND POLISHING

Even if you don't want your pieces to look super shiny, you should still finish your piece so all the scratches are removed and your pieces are soft and comfortable to wear.

Polishing Cloth

Use a polishing cloth to lightly shine a piece. These are especially handy at craft and trade shows to brighten up your work. These cloths are inexpensive and are very useful to have around.

Polishing Wheel

A polishing wheel is a rotary tool with a steel spindle that fits on a variety of wheels to finish, polish, or even grind pieces. As you do when operating all machinery, wear safety goggles, tie your hair back, and don't wear loose-fitting clothing when you're working on the polishing wheel. Never polish chains on a wheel: it is a safety hazard and they can get stuck in the machine.

Polishing Compounds

Purchase a muslin or felt wheel to attach to your spindle. You can also purchase a tapered inside polisher to attach to the spindle to polish the inside of rings. The wheel doesn't polish your piece; the compound that you put on it does. A polishing compound is like a clay mixed with grit to take out scratches and polish your piece. If you are working with multiple types of compounds, designate a wheel for each one and don't cross contaminate. Always wash your piece well in between using polishing compounds. There are hundreds of types of polishing compounds that do different things. Cutting compounds, sometimes called *prepolish*, are fairly abrasive and remove any leftover scratches as the final stages of finishing. Rouge is a very popular high-polish compound that will make your pieces very shiny. Compounds are also manufactured specifically for gold, platinum, or even for softer gemstones.

You can also use the polishing wheel to put other types of finishes on your work. Get a matte wheel to achieve a flat finish or a brushed wheel to create fine lines for a brushed finish.

POLISHING WITH A TUMBLER

Use a tumbler to polish many pieces at the same time. This is a great way to speed up production and achieve consistent finishes on your jewelry. Tumbling will not just polish but also work harden and clean your pieces. You can oxidize your jewelry before putting it in the tumbler to achieve a gunmetal finish. Make sure to run a cleansing cycle (page 65) before putting nonoxidized pieces in, or have a separate tumbler for this. Use steel shot for a high-shine finish and plastic shot for a matte finish. I like to use a mixture of the two for a semipolished look.

LOST-WAX CASTING

This is a process in which a molten metal is poured into a temporary mold that was made by a wax model. It's a widely used production process for jewelry and other industries. Casting is an extremely efficient process for production. By creating molds of your prototypes, you can replicate the piece over and over again in many different types of metals.

Lost-Wax Casting Process

CREATE A PROTOTYPE

Create your prototype, sometimes referred to as the model, from carving wax, metal, or a natural object. Your master piece should be perfect, with all scratches removed and every aspect of your design in line with how you want the final piece to look like. Place, or have your model maker place, a wax sprue on your model; this acts as the passageway for the metal to flow into your piece. Depending on the size and shape of your piece, one or more sprues are usually placed on the thickest part of your model. If you have a ring with texture, you can place the sprue on the inside of the ring. Once the piece is cast in metal, the sprue is cut off, sanded, and finished so you can no longer see it. If your model maker or caster is putting the sprue on, request a specific place that goes well with your design, and always ask the expert's advice.

As a general rule for casting, keep in mind that 1 millimeter is the thinnest you should go. You can get away with casting thinner than that, but if you go any thinner than 0.5 millimeters, you will have trouble with your metal flowing.

MOLD MAKING

Create a mold of your prototype. This is the most efficient way to make duplicates of your jewelry from the same model. You can learn mold making yourself or use a professional mold maker. Most casting houses

have at least one mold maker on staff. Good-quality molds are just as important as the prototype itself. Depending on the material and thickness of your prototype, have a rubber or silicone mold made. There are many types of molds, but rubber and silicone are the most common. Molds can tear and break and generally do not last forever. Be sure to keep your prototypes somewhere safe, and certainly do not sell them! They are your master copies, and if your mold breaks, you have the original model on hand to create another one. Molds start at around $15 and go up in price based on size.

If you want to make molds of natural objects, like sea shells and animal bones, consider learning how to make your own one- or two-part molds. You can make a mold of a natural object, pour wax into it, and then create a wax model around it. This way you can add jump rings or turn that natural object into a piece of jewelry without having to get a professional mold made first.

THE TWO MOST COMMONLY USED TYPES OF MOLDS:

Natural Rubber Mold: This has the longest life of any molds and has high tear and tensile strength. This was an industry standard for decades, so most mold makers are very familiar with it. Rubber molds will tear the least and last the longest, and can be used thousands of times without breaking apart. Your model will be placed inside the rubber and then put into a vulcanizer to get all the air and bubbles out. The mold is then cut in half to reveal a perfect negative space of your model. Since this process is vulcanized, something fragile like a wax model or natural object will not withstand the process. Use this type of mold for a metal model only. The shrinkage rate with a natural rubber mold can be up to 4 percent, and this should be taken into consideration when you're designing your piece.

Silicone Mold: This type of mold has a shorter shelf life than natural rubber and can be used a few hundred times without breaking apart, but has a higher-quality surface finish and will get you more detail. Liquid silicone is poured over your model, which is placed inside a square plastic mold. The silicone hardens at room temperature and then is cut in half to reveal a perfect negative space of your model. Since this process is cured at room temperature, it works great with wax models or more fragile designs. The shrinkage rate with silicone molds can be virtually unnoticeable or up to 3 percent, so be sure to ask your mold maker about this.

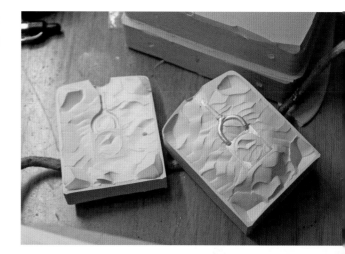

You may cast your wax model straight to metal, called straight casting, and then finish your metal casting by sanding and polishing the piece. Your metal casting will now become your master piece, which you can now take a mold of. This is a great option if you are new to wax carving or want to take an extra step in perfecting

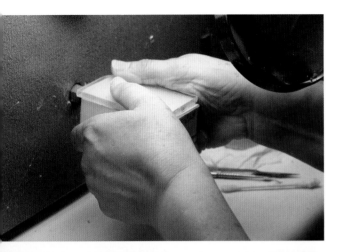

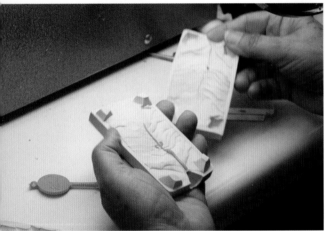

The waxes are then built to form "trees," and each wax tree is cast in one type of metal. Your wax models, which you can think of as the leaves, are placed on a thick wax rod, which you can think of as the tree trunk. This rod is attached to a rubber base. The sprue on your wax model, which you can think of as the branch, is connected to the center wax trunk using a heated electric wax pen to slightly melt them together. All of the waxes on this tree will get cast in the same metal.

A metal flask is placed around your wax tree and secured to the rubber base. An investment, a compound similar to liquid plaster that can withstand the high heat of molten metal, is poured on top of the wax tree, filling to the top of the flask. The investment then hardens overnight. Once hardened, the rubber base is removed to reveal an opening leading to the tree.

your model. Have waxes injected into your mold using a wax injector machine. A wax injector heats wax to around 160°F (71°C), depending on what type of wax you are using, and is pressurized to shoot the liquid wax into your mold. As the liquid wax fills the negative space to form a positive, this creates a perfect replica of your original model.

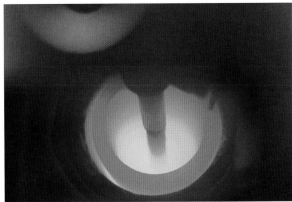

The flask is placed inside a kiln, allowing the wax tree to melt out and leaving behind a perfect negative space. When the flask is at the appropriate temperature for the molten metal, it is placed inside a vacuum or centrifuge caster. Molten metal is then poured into the opening, flowing from the trunk to the branches to the leaves. The flask is allowed to cool for about fifteen minutes, and then submerged in water to allow the investment to shoot out, revealing the metal tree.

Each piece is cut off the tree at the sprue, or branch, and then weighed. The cost is calculated by the market price of the metal multiplied by the weight of the piece. A labor charge is added onto each piece, starting as low as 50¢ per piece, depending on the size and complexity of

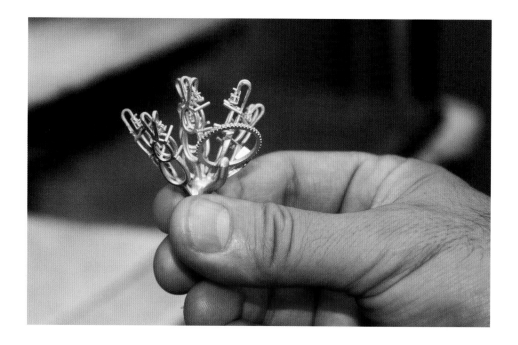

the design. The excess metal is then sent to a refinery and recycled to be used again.

The casting will then be cleaned, which involves cutting the sprue off, grinding away the excess metal, sanding the whole piece with coarse then fine sandpaper, and then finally polishing it (see metal finishing on page 80).

Metals You Can Cast for Jewelry

You can cast in precious metals like platinum, palladium, all alloys of gold, fine silver, and sterling silver. Check with your caster as to what kind of alloys the company has available and if the company offers recycled metals. If you are casting your pieces in recycled metals, request a copy of the certificate of the metal makeup to keep on file if a customer ever asks for proof that the metal you used was recycled.

As a less expensive option, you can cast in base metals like brass, bronze, and stainless steel. You can plate a thin layer of metal on top of these or leave them raw. More and more designers are making jewelry in brass or bronze without plating it, since the price of precious metals is rising.

If you're designing costume jewelry, consider casting your work in white metal, an alloy of tin, zinc, cadmium, and other inexpensive metals. White metal has a very low melting temperature and is cast between 450°F and 575°F (232–302°C). Since the melting point is low, compared to other metals, the white metal is poured directly into a two-part rubber mold. The metal is poured into one part of a round rubber mold, which resembles a large round pancake, and then the second part is placed on top to create the shape. After the pieces are finished, the components are then plated with a very thin layer of metal, such as gold or silver.

ESTIMATING METAL PRICE

Get in the habit of weighing your wax model so you can estimate how much the piece will cost when it is cast in metal. Weigh your wax on a scale set to pennyweight, sometimes abbreviated as "pwt" or "dwt." Multiply the wax weight by the specific gravity of the metal you are casting in to calculate how much your model will weigh in metal. Then multiply the metal weight by the price of the metal to estimate the cost. If you plan to do a lot of work by casting, keep a list of your wax weights so you can easily calculate how much a specific piece will cost in different

metals. This will make customer inquiries easy to answer without guessing.

Specific gravity is the ratio of how dense a substance is compared to a reference substance, which is usually water. Every substance on our planet has its own density. If you have the exact same casting in both sterling silver and platinum, the platinum piece weighs more because the substance is more dense, even though they're the same exact size.

(Wax weight x Specific gravity) =
Weight in metal x Metal price = Cost

Here's an example (also see below): We have a wax-carved ring that weighs 0.5 dwt and we want to estimate how much the piece will cost in sterling silver. Since precious metals are commodities, their prices fluctuate daily. You can find the daily price of metals online, or call your caster and ask. For this example, we are going to estimate that the market price of sterling silver for the day is $1.91 per pennyweight. Remember when estimating your cost that there will be a labor fee tagged on to each piece.

Wax weight	x	Specific gravity =	Weight in metal	x	Metal price = Cost
0.5 dwt	x	10.4 =	5.2 dwt	x	$1.91 = $9.93

SPECIFIC GRAVITY FOR THE MOST COMMON CAST METALS FOR JEWELRY

Symbol	Metal	Melting Temperature Celsius/Fahrenheit	Specific Gravity
220	Brass	1044 / 1910	8.8
511	Bronze	1060 / 1945	8.8
Au	Fine Gold	1063 / 1945	19.3
920	22K Yellow Gold	977 / 1790	17.3
750	18K Yellow Gold	882 / 1620	15.5
750	18K Green Gold	966 / 1770	15.6
750	18K Rose Gold	932 / 1719	15.5
750	18K White Gold	904 / 1660	15.5
580	14K Yellow Gold	802 / 1476	13.4
580	14K Green Gold	735 / 1535	13.6
580	14K Rose Gold	827 / 1520	13.4
580	14K White Gold	927 / 1700	13.7
420	10K Yellow Gold	876 / 1609	11.6
420	10K Green Gold	804 / 1480	11.6
420	10K Rose Gold	710 / 1490	11.7
420	10K White Gold	927 / 1760	11.6
Pd	Palladium	1549 / 2820	12.2
Pt	Platinum	1774 / 3225	21.4
Ag	Fine Silver	961 / 1762	10.6
925	Sterling Silver	920 / 1640	10.4
–	Stainless Steel	1371 / 2500	7.8

METAL PLATING AND GOLD FILLED

Plating a thin coating of metal over base metals is a great way to offer gold or silver pieces at a much lower price. You can also come up with fun and trendy colors by plating with metals like gunmetal, brass, and copper. Gold-filled metals offer another way to create gold pieces that you can sell at a lower price.

ELECTROPLATING

Base metals are immersed in a liquid containing chemically bound gold particles, which are electrically charged onto the base. Electroplating also works with silver, rhodium, gunmetal, and other metals. The plated metal must be at least 7 millimeters thick (7/1,000,000 inch). This is a great option for plating jewelry so the surface will not wear off too quickly. Keep in mind that any electroplated piece that has contact with your skin, like the inside of a ring or the back of a chain, will wear off more quickly than a piece without electroplating.

Flash Plating

This the same process as electroplating, but the particles are less than 7 millimeters thick (7/1,000,000 inch). Flash plating is often done to add a decorative accent, creating a two-tone look on a piece of jewelry.

Vermeil

Gold plating over sterling silver is referred to in the jewelry industry as *vermeil*. Vermeil can be a good selling point because once the gold plating wears off, there is still precious metal underneath.

Rhodium Plating

Rhodium is a member of the platinum family but is harder and whiter. Most white precious metals used in commercial fine jewelry, like white gold, platinum, and palladium, are plated with rhodium so they appear brighter. This is a jewelry industry standard, but not something you have to follow.

Gold Filled

In this process, a thick layer of gold is mechanically bonded to a base metal and fused by heat and pressure. The layer of gold is thicker than it is in plating; you can purchase gold-filled chains and findings. You can also purchase gold-filled wire and sheet to fabricate jewelry. Dissolve 50 percent borax into 50 percent denatured alcohol to use as flux while soldering, and use gold or gold-filled solder. Store this solution in an air-tight jar, and add denatured alcohol as needed if it evaporates.

IN-HOUSE PRODUCTION

Depending on your skills, design, and studio setup, you may choose to do all your own production. This will work well for a small-scale production with one person. Alternatively, you can bring on other bench jewelers to join your team. Even if you are the only one on your production line at the moment, establish good habits regarding record keeping and production systems to make seamless transitions as you expand.

As your business grows, you may need help keeping up with orders or freeing up

things that take up your time when you could be focusing on designing, selling, and making your jewelry. Be sure to check local labor laws about having an intern work in your space.

I offer a three-month seasonal internship program in my studio. I have had as interns college students or people who are interested in learning about jewelry design and how a small craft company works. I provide a daily lunch and travel stipend and encourage my interns to ask me questions about the business. Then I give them feedback at the end of the internship to help them grow.

your own time so you can focus on other aspects of running the business. Remember that growing pains are healthy and are a great problem to have. Try to focus on what aspects of the business you do best and what you can delegate to someone else.

Internship Program

Hiring an intern is a great way to gain some extra help in exchange for a valuable learning experience. Reach out to a career center at a local college or craft school and let them know what you have available. Focus your internship on one aspect of the business, such as assembling jewelry, or graphic design, or have the person shadow you to get a well-rounded experience of all aspects of running a small crafts business.

Make a list of responsibilities an intern can handle. Think about the most basic

Bench Jeweler or Assistant

For more professional help, hire a bench jeweler to assist you in your studio on a freelance basis when you need the extra help, part time or full time. Contact a college or trade school with an art program or ask for referrals from other local jewelers.

Have your bench jeweler handle basic tasks involved in the production of your jewelry line. Break steps down and have your bench jeweler work in assembly-line fashion to accomplish the tasks faster and more efficiently. If she is cleaning fifty castings, cut all fifty sprues at once, grind all fifty pieces at once, sand all fifty pieces at once, and so on.

When the workload slows down, have your bench jeweler work on building inventory of your best-selling items or prep things for future orders, like assembling chains. Be patient and make sure you communicate clearly with bench jewelers. The pieces they are making are your designs, so be sure to break down the steps and tell them exactly how you want each one made and how the final product should look.

Hire an assistant to help with sales, marketing, and administrative tasks to free up your time so you can focus on making your jewelry. Create a task schedule for short-term and long-term projects for the assistant to work on. Make sure to tell her how to write and speak about your work. Language is very important in building a brand and telling a story, so make sure you are both on the same page.

At different times in my life as a jewelry designer, I have found myself at various points along this spectrum—the bench jeweler who is producing someone else's designs, the production manager of a jewelry company overseeing a team of bench jewelers, the marketing and administrative assistant running the business and communicating with clients, and, finally, the designer who is having bench jewelers produce her designs and assistants helping with marketing and administration.

Mistakes happen when you don't communicate with one another. Keep in mind that every jeweler has his own way of making things, so be very clear about how you want something done. The most difficult aspect of being a bench jeweler can be making and finishing pieces in someone else's style.

OUT-OF-HOUSE PRODUCTION

You may choose to outsource some or all of your production depending on your skill levels and the volume of orders you have. There are a vast amount of vendors worldwide who specialize in specific techniques, and small and large companies who do every aspect from start to finish. Most large cities have a jewelry district—some bigger than others—that can handle jobs small and large. To avoid miscommunication, aim to keep your production as close to you as possible. As you have more demand for your jewelry and you need extra help, outsource parts or all of the work to a local industry. If vendors aren't available locally, many companies ship worldwide. The best way to find resources is through referrals from other designers or vendors you already work with. Visit industry trade shows like the MJSA Show, the JA Show, and the Gem and Mineral Show to make new contacts. (See the resource list on page 167.)

Contracting Work Out

To make your production more efficient, contract out specific jobs that you don't need to do yourself. Contracting out specific jobs may be more cost-effective if the contractor can make more pieces faster and of better quality than you can. Use specific people for each job, or find someone who will do multiple aspects of the production work for you. If you are using many vendors in the same area, ask if one will drop off finished pieces at the next place or hire a messenger service to save you some time.

MODEL MAKERS

Work with a jeweler or a professional model maker to make the prototypes of your designs. Contact a local jeweler to see if she is interested, or ask if she can refer you to someone. Show her sketches, renderings, or pictures of what you are looking for. The more information you offer her, the easier her job bringing your designs to life will be.

CASTING HOUSES

Use a casting company to create multiples of your pieces. Find a company that does good-quality work and is easy to communicate with. You can keep all your molds on file at your casting company and email your orders over. If you don't have a casting company close by, find one in a nearby city and have the company ship your castings to you.

Some casting companies offer finishing services as well. They will cut off sprues, finish castings, polish, and even oxidize your work. You can get one or all of these services done for an extra fee. Give the company copies of your spec sheets and a finished sample for employees to reference. Keep in mind that people in the industry often have their own way of finishing pieces, so take the time to explain what you want. This is a great way to speed up production so you can focus on other aspects of the business.

METAL FABRICATION, FINISHING, AND POLISHING

Contract out fabrication and finishing work to a jeweler or a finishing company. Show fabricators and finishers spec sheets and finished pieces so they know exactly how your pieces should look. Bring your pieces to a polisher to shine them so you can skip that step. The more professionally you act, the more professionally they will treat you.

STONE SETTING

Work with a stone setter to set your gemstones securely and inexpensively. Most setting jobs will cost under $10 and this is a simple thing to outsource. Some stone setters have small diamonds on hand, but I suggest supplying your own gemstones so you can be sure of the quality and consistency. Mark your piece with a permanent marker in the exact spot where you want your stone set. If you don't know how to set stones, talk with your setter and ask if he has any suggestions on how to make your model better. Reach out to local jewelers to see if they offer stone-setting services or if they can give you a recommendation of someone who does.

METAL PLATING

Plating equipment can be tremendously expensive, so definitely consider sourcing this out. Talk to your plater about metal options and thicknesses. If you don't have a local plating company in your area, send your pieces to a large plating company where you probably will get better prices. Plating is generally less expensive when done in larger batches, so be conscious of this when sending out work to be plated to avoid overpaying.

WHERE TO FIND CONTRACTORS

The easiest way to find new contractors is to ask for referrals. Ask your friends who they like to use, and ask your vendors if they have any recommendations. Some helpful resources are listed on page 167.

Check out jewelry industry trade shows to find new vendors. Casting companies, refineries, metal platers, chain and finding companies, gemstone dealers, and other vendors attend trade shows throughout North America and internationally to make new contacts. Some trade shows to look into are the MJSA Show, the JA Show, and the Gem and Mineral Show.

To find out about sources and trade shows, join a local, national, or international jewelry guild. Etsy has a lot of great groups you can join that offer support for one another. Some other groups to look into are the Society of North American Goldsmiths (SNAG), Ethical Metalsmiths, Women's Jewelry Association (WJA), and the Enamelist Society.

FACTORY PRODUCTION

For a large-scale production line, you may choose to have all steps of production done under the same roof at a factory. The minimums for this type of production are usually very high, making it more cost-effective for both parties. Generally speaking, the more pieces you are ordering at once, the less costly the order is. Try to work with a vendor who is as close to you as possible. Besides supporting local businesses, the closer you are to your vendors, the more involved you can be in the decision-making processes. The farther away you are, the more you have to pay in shipping costs, and there may be little to no face-to-face communication.

PRODUCTION LINE TIPS AND TRICKS

Work in an Assembly Line Fashion

When making jewelry for a production line, think of yourself as an assembly line. If you are working on ten simple wire rings, work on all ten at the same time, as opposed to each one from start to finish. This method makes you work faster and more efficiently.

Cut all ten pieces of wire to the correct length, file all edges of the wire, anneal all wires at the same time, form all wires into the required shape and make ends meet for soldering, solder all seams and pickle, form all into the final shape with a ring mandrel and a plastic hammer, sand all rings with coarse then fine sandpaper, and polish all rings.

Focus on Efficiency over Design

When producing a jewelry line, focus on efficiency over design. That doesn't mean you have to make simple pieces. Rather, it means you need to perfect your designs in your prototype, or your model. Break down the steps of creating the piece and see how you can make it faster and more easily while still achieving the same end result.

Consider incorporating premade settings instead of constructing each one by hand. Purchase calibrated gemstones, so they are all exactly the same size, to make setting your stones easier. If you can't find what you are looking for or have a specific shape and cut designed, use a lapidary, or a gemstone cutter, to customize them for you.

Use manufactured chain and findings instead of making them yourself. Better yet, look into finished chains, with the findings already assembled and soldered. Chain and finding companies offer a wide variety of chains in base metals and precious metals. Most companies will take custom orders to create finished chains if the order is large enough.

Use the same mold and castings for multiple pieces. For example, if you have a mold of a bezel setting with a jump ring attached, parallel to the piece, get five pieces cast. Two settings will be assembled with earring wires for dangle earrings. One setting will be assembled with a jump ring attached to a finished chain for a simple pendant. One setting will get the jump ring cut off and soldered to a simple wire ring. One setting will get the jump ring cut off and soldered to a simple wire bangle. Now you have four pieces of jewelry that came from the same mold and will get set with the same gemstone to make a small collection.

Everything you can do by hand, you can do on a machine faster. A flexible shaft will be your greatest tool for working more efficiently and faster. Use it to grind away sprues, sand, and soften.

Cutting

The more you use your jeweler's saw, the better you will get with it. If you're cutting shapes out of metal sheet, make sure you're using the appropriate blade size. The thicker the piece of metal, the thicker the blade. Buy your saw blades by the gross (144) instead of by the dozen (12). If you cut out intricate patterns and shapes in your sheet metal, look into getting your shapes laser-cut out of sheet metal to save time.

Filing

Instead of filing every edge of sheet metal after cutting, put it in a rotary tumbler for at least six hours, or overnight. This will soften all of the edges so they're not sharp, polish your pieces, and work harden them.

Sanding

Use a flex shaft to sand your pieces with coarse then fine sandpapers, instead of sanding by hand. Use a bur, like a split mandrel, to sand your pieces faster. Insert a 6-inch (15-cm) strip of sandpaper the same width as the opening. When you press on the pedal, the sandpaper will wrap itself around the bur. This is great because you can quickly change your sandpaper grit without changing burs. Try taping down your sandpaper if you don't like it flapping around.

Polishing

Instead of polishing each piece by hand, invest in a tumbler to polish your pieces in large batches. I like to tumble my pieces overnight so they come out bright, shiny, and work hardened in the morning. Don't tumble pieces with soft stones set in them, but harder stones like diamonds, sapphires, and rubies should be okay. Always tumble a test batch for twenty minutes if you are unsure how it will do in the tumbler. Separate oxidized pieces and non-oxidized pieces in different tumblers to avoid contaminating the machine. If your tumbler gets contaminated, run a rinse cycle of 50 percent white distilled vinegar and 50 percent water for twenty minutes, followed by a twenty-minute cycle with water covering the shot and 1 tablespoon (15 ml) of baking soda.

CHAPTER 5

Marketing Your Jewelry Line

✦

WEBSITES

It is imperative to have a website if you are running a business these days. In today's world, everything is available at your fingertips. If you don't have a website, people can't find information abut you and your work. It is extremely important to have a website to represent yourself not just as an artist and designer, but also as a business person.

Purchasing a Domain Name and Web Hosting

Purchasing your domain name is simple. Go to a website like Domain.com and use the search bar to see what's available. Purchase a domain name by paying a yearly rental fee.

Web hosting is a business that gives you space and manages storage for your website. Think of this as paying to rent a storage unit online. These days most web hosting companies offer web hosting and domain purchasing all in one.

DIY Websites

Share inspirations, photographs of your work, and event information, many of which you can do right from your smartphone using today's tools. Use a platform like a Facebook page or a blog, a DIY website or a professionally built e-commerce site.

Build your own website by using one of the many template-based website companies. Websites like Squarespace, Wix, and GoDaddy make it very easy to build an attractive website without knowing how to code. Most importantly, post beautiful

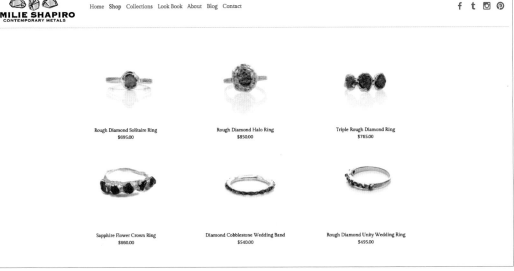

Rough Diamond Solitaire Ring
$695.00

Rough Diamond Halo Ring
$850.00

Triple Rough Diamond Ring
$765.00

Sapphire Flower Crown Ring
$660.00

Diamond Cobblestone Wedding Band
$540.00

Rough Diamond Unity Wedding Ring
$495.00

images and strong content about your work. Keep it simple! Most template-based companies have built-in e-commerce features to make selling your products online a cinch. Make sure to activate social sharing options so viewers can easily share your work with their networks.

What Information to Put on Your Website

ABOUT THE ARTIST

Have a page dedicated to telling your story. Share your inspiration, how you got into making jewelry, and your company ethos.

CONTACT INFORMATION

At the very least, have your contact information available so customers can reach out to you. You may have one or multiple email addresses, depending on a person's inquiry.

Share your social media handles with a link that opens a new window to your page. Be sure to have at least one area on your website for a viewer to sign up for your mailing list.

FAQS

Consider including a frequently asked questions (FAQ) section to your site to answer questions you get all time about materials, production time, custom orders, and shipping.

RETAILERS

If your jewelry is sold at retail stores, have a page listing the store information. Sometimes people call these "stockists." List the store name and location. You can link to each store's website if you wish, but make sure the link opens in a new window.

WHOLESALE

If you sell your work wholesale, have some information about how a store can get in touch with you if they are interested in carrying your line, what information they should provide to you, and where they can see your work. If you have a sales representative, a showroom, or participate in wholesale trade shows, include that information here.

EVENTS

If you have any upcoming events, like trunk shows, craft shows, or a sale, share that information so people know how and where to purchase your designs.

PRESS

Share any press or awards you've received on a designated page. You can create a slideshow of press clippings or simply a list with links. Don't be shy: if you've been recognized, let people know about it!

BLOG

Have a blog that is part of your website, as opposed to one that redirects visitors to another site. This is a great way for admirers and customers to read about your inspirations, to learn about your process, and to get to know your brand. People can also find your website by searching for the things you are blogging about. Publish your blog posts on your social media networks to encourage other people to share them.

POLICIES

Post your policies, including deposits for custom work and return policy, on your website to avoid confusion or customer complaints.

RETURN POLICY

Establish a return policy and specify it on all your materials, including your website, so customers are aware of it before they make a purchase. It is up to you to decide what kind of return policy to put in place. Consider a return window, or options to exchange a piece for credit toward another piece. If you sell your work through retailers, be sure to note that you cannot accept returns for any pieces purchased from a retailer. The piece must be returned to the retailer.

REPAIR POLICY

Establish a repair and ring-sizing policy. If something breaks, you should fix it and figure out why it broke. I offer complimentary ring sizing and repair, but the customer has to pay for shipping. I find this encourages customers to purchase a ring with confidence, knowing it can be adjusted if needed.

CUSTOM WORK

If you do custom work, let people know about it and about how they can get in touch with you to set up an in-person or virtual appointment. Make your payment options clear. For instance, you might require a 50 percent deposit at the beginning of the design process and the balance on completion.

MATERIAL INFORMATION

Specify your material information and let people know if it is recycled, fair trade, or contains nickel or any other allergen. If you work with unplated brass, bronze, or copper, you may want to point out that these materials can turn skin a greenish color, depending on the wearer's body chemistry, but the green tinge is not harmful and washes right off.

PRODUCTION AND DELIVERY TIME

Establish a production window, depending on whether the requested piece is in stock or made to order. Let customers know approximately how long pieces will take to produce and ship out.

SHIPPING OPTIONS AND COST

Specify your shipping options, pricing, and what carrier you use. If you have a rush option, let customers know that and what the extra fee is. Consider offering a gift-wrapping option.

E-commerce Shop

In our globalized world, it's easy to sell and buy products from all around the globe. If you are designing your website through a platform-based company, most likely the company will have an option for e-commerce already built in. If your website does not offer this option, look into e-commerce sites like BigCartel, Shopify, or Yahoo Small Business.

When designing an e-commerce platform to sell your products, one of the most important things is to have good-quality product shots of your jewelry and clear product information. You might have beautiful jewelry, but with poor-quality images your pieces will not sell. (See photography tips on page 12). You can arrange the products by type—rings, bracelets, necklaces, earrings—for an easy shopping experience. Aim to have images of the front, top, and side views of your piece on a white background. You may also want model shots to show the jewelry on a person, which helps buyers visualize what the piece will look like on them. Make sure to have a short description of the piece, materials, size options, availability, and dimensions.

Product Name: Enchanted Forest Earrings

Description: Watermelon tourmaline slices are surrounded by pink sapphires set in recycled 14K yellow gold. French earring wires give this piece movement and security.

This piece is made to order. Allow 2–3 weeks to ship.

Dimensions: 1" L x 3/4" W

Third-Party Websites

Many websites, like CustomMade.com, Strolby.com, and Etsy.com, are geared toward handmade items. They make it easy to list your products to sell. Some have monthly or yearly subscriptions, and some charge per product listed. This is a great way to join an existing online community where customers are already going to shop for products like yours.

Etsy is the best-known website for selling your work to retail customers. It is very simple to make up a profile and upload photographs and product information, and it costs only a few cents to list each product. You already have consumers visiting Etsy seeking handmade, quality items not found at a big box store. Etsy is a handmade brand itself and a great place to sell your work exclusively or in addition to your own e-commerce website. The site also has very helpful forums and resources about everything to do with creating, selling, and marketing handmade jewelry on Etsy.

Professionally Built Websites

You can hire a web designer to build you a website using a template or a customized site. Having a customized site built can be extremely pricey, costing upwards of tens of thousands of dollars. I don't recommend getting a website built for you right away, since there are so many easy and less expensive options.

Ask a college student who is looking to build his portfolio to either build you a website or help build one for you. Be very clear about what you want and give him page information, copy, and images that you want to use.

Website Design

When you are designing a website for the first time, a good exercise is to use an index card for each page you plan to build. Each index card will represent an individual page. Here you can write down the key points you want to have on each page and what images you would like to include. Now arrange the index cards so you can see the order of the pages and any subpages that connect together. These are referred to as parent and child pages. This will be especially useful if you're working with a web designer so you know how many pages need to be designed.

EMAIL MARKETING

Email marketing is an effective way to stay in touch with customers and build a relationship. Have an email list exclusively for retail customers. Use free email programs, like MailChimp or Constant Contact, to send clean, formatted emails and be able to see reports. These programs offer reports about who opened your emails and which products they clicked on so you can gain a sense of which products elicit the greatest interest. I like to send out email blasts bimonthly through most of the year, and once a week during the holiday season. Highlight different jewelry pieces or collections, let customers know about upcoming trunk shows or craft markets where you'll be appearing, and include any other exciting news you have to share.

Have at least one area on your website with the option to sign up for your mailing list. I like to offer an incentive of 10 percent off customers' first order when they join the list. Keep in mind that people are trusting you with their contact information, so don't bombard their inbox with messages and don't give away or sell customer information.

SOCIAL MEDIA

Social media is an extremely effective way to market your pieces for free and build brand awareness. You can build a visual story of your brand by posting images of work in progress, inspiration pictures, and finished pieces. This is a great way to invite customers into your world and make them fall in love with your brand.

Because there are so many platforms to choose from, and they are constantly changing and being updated, establishing a presence on social media can feel overwhelming. Among the most popular platforms are Instagram, Facebook, Twitter, Tumblr, and Pinterest. If you are new to social media, pick one to focus on and connect it to your other channels so they automatically share. I put my energy into Instagram; I find it easy to navigate from my smartphone and aim to post one picture a day of a piece in progress, finished products, or inspiration photos. This helps potential customers visualize my brand and see the handmade process behind the scenes.

When I post photos, they are connected to my Twitter, Tumblr, and Facebook accounts. This helps me maintain a social media presence in under five minutes a day.

If you'll be appearing at an upcoming craft show or trade show, tag the show's social media handle. Use the show's designated hashtag to make it easy for buyers and press to find out about your brand. I often post inspiration and in-process pictures, which help people understand my brand, validate that it is handmade, and see the story behind it.

Use hashtags so people can find you. This way you'll gain new followers. Hashtags are essentially keywords. If you click on a hashtag, it will bring up all the public posts that have that hashtag. Establish a hashtag for your brand, like #EmilieShapiroJewelry, and encourage customers to share photos wearing your jewelry. See what hashtags other designers in your category and people with similar interest are using to help widen your following.

When sharing content on social media, remember that anyone can access it. Consider watermarking your images with your company name, logo, or website so no matter where it ends up, the viewer can see who the owner is. Always have your posts redirect to your website. Include a link to a specific product or place on your website to promote traffic back to your site.

As your company grows, you may consider investing more time and energy into social media, but this is a great way to start. To manage all your social media on one page, use a service like Hootsuite. It's easy to schedule updates and engage with followers all on one platform.

Paid Advertising

Most social media platforms are now offering paid promotional options. These allow you to test out paid marketing without spending a fortune. Try promoting your jewelry Facebook page or promoting a few of your jewelry images on Pinterest. Make sure all your posts link back to your website. You can invest $20 in a paid promotion, and if you feel it was successful, try it again.

If you're exhibiting at a trade show, you may consider paying to advertise in the show directory or a gift guide geared toward buyers like *Retailing Insight* or *Niche* magazine. Trade shows often have display cases in the entrance area that you can pay to show your pieces in.

CROSS PROMOTION

Cross promotion is a terrific way to gain more followers and boost brand awareness. Cross promotion is when you promote another brand, either one that you own or someone else's, while you promote yours.

Here Are Some Examples:

Say you are exhibiting at a craft show where a few of your friends are showing their work as well. On your display table you have a ceramic bowl, handmade by one of your friends, holding some of your designs. It looks really beautiful with your jewelry and you are promoting your friend's work. On her display table, meanwhile, she has a piece of your jewelry sitting on one of her ring stands, and she is promoting your work.

Your jewelry was used in a photo shoot, and when the photographer posts a photograph from the shoot, she tags you and all the other designers involved. All the designers repost the photo and tag everyone involved in the shoot.

PRESS

Press coverage is a great way to get your brand to reach more people and build brand awareness. If a stylist or editorial coordinator requests to pull some of your pieces for a photo shoot or event, make sure to request an LOR, or letter of responsibility, and include a loan form with the pieces you are lending out. An LOR will come from the stylist or company requesting to borrow your work stating they are responsible for any work lost, stolen, or damaged while in their care. A loan form is a detailed list of the work you are lending out including product name, description, and full retail price. Be sure to include your contact information, the address they should be returned to, the date the pieces were loaned, and the date they should be returned (see example on page 105).

Reaching Out to Bloggers

Reach out to bloggers you like to follow on social media. Lend or gift them a piece of your jewelry in exchange for having them review

EMILIE SHAPIRO
CONTEMPORARY METALS

Emilie Shapiro Contemporary Metals
43-01 21st Street, No. 312B
Long Island City, NY 11101
press@emilieshapiro.com
555-555-5555

Pulled by: [Name of company]
Sent to: [Address of company]
Date: [Date items shipped]
Return Date: [Date items should be returned]

ITEM	DESCRIPTION	QTY	PRICE
1. chakra bangle ruby	brass, raw ruby	1	$90
2. chakra bangle sapphire	brass, raw sapphire	1	$90
3. mosaic wide cuff	brass, raw emerald	1	$150
4. mosaic double earrings	brass, silver, raw emerald	1	$82
5. mosaic small earrings	brass, silver, raw emerald	1	$55
6. mosaic triple ring	brass, raw emerald	1	$75
7. mosaic single ring	brass, raw emerald	1	$60
8. mosaic double ring	brass, raw emerald	1	$55
9. mosaic wilted ring	brass, raw emerald	1	$65
10. mosaic winged pendant	brass, raw emerald	1	$125
11. mosaic little necklace	brass, raw emerald	1	$55
12. mosaic v pendant	brass, raw emerald	1	$95
13. mosaic shield	brass, emerald	1	$125
14. water waves arm piece	brass	1	$175
15. wide wilted cuff	bronze	1	$95
Merchandise loan total		**15**	**$1,392**

[Name of person responsible] of [Name of company] takes full responsibility for any damage caused by any individual involved in this project to the pieces provided by Emilie Shapiro Contemporary Metals. [Name of company] will be invoiced for the full retail price for any missing and damaged pieces.

it on their social media outlets. Bloggers with both big and small sites are always looking for new products to review and talk about.

Reaching Out to Editors

Even if you don't have any press connections, reaching out to editors can be simple if you do a little research. Look at the credits on a website or magazine for the accessories editor. Send her an email introducing yourself and your brand with an image inserted in the email.

You may consider gifting a few pieces of jewelry to a select group of editors, as they are always looking for new products to feature. Send them a piece of jewelry in your packaging with some marketing material included. Write a note introducing yourself and encourage them to wear it around. Be sure to include your contact information so they can get in touch with you. June is a great time to gift editors a piece, as they are planning for holiday issues and gift guides.

CHAPTER 6

How and Where to Sell
Your Jewelry Line

✦

There are two basic ways to sell your work—retail, which is selling directly to the public, or wholesale, which is selling in bulk to a store. Each method has advantages and disadvantages, and you don't need to focus on just one. Figuring out what works best for you depends on the product you make and the quantities you can produce. One-of-a-kind items and part-time production crafts may do better selling directly to retail channels, at craft markets, and online. A full-time production craft business will be most successful selling wholesale to shops, catalogs, and e-commerce sites.

If you have never sold your jewelry before and are looking for a big push, give yourself a deadline. Plan a jewelry party or sign up for a craft fair so you have a deadline that you need to meet. It's not going to be perfect the first time; there will be a lot of things you forget and things you will wish you had done differently. Take notes in a journal the whole time, learn from your mistakes, and assess how you can improve for the next time.

RETAIL

Retail refers to selling a product from a fixed location or an online shop, in small quantities or individual pieces for direct consumption by the purchaser. You can retail your work at a variety of outlets— a private studio, a brick-and-mortar store, an online web store, or a craft fair. Selling your work directly to the public is a great way to get started in a jewelry business part time. If you are selling direct retail, you have to do a lot of legwork to sell at markets, you need to have inventory to sell, and you have to make enough sales for it to be worthwhile.

Selling Directly from Your Studio

Take appointments or invite clients to view your collection. This works well if you're creating custom pieces and the customer wants to work with you on design. Many urban areas have a designated time of year for open studios or other arts events. When foot traffic is higher, this is a great time to invite people to see your work in your studio or have a sale. Some areas have "First Fridays" or another time designated for galleries and studios to open their doors and encourage people to come in. Contact the organizer of these events to see if you can get on the website or the map of participants.

Jewelry Parties

This is not a new concept, but events like Tupperware parties have always been really effective. Ask a friend or family member to host a party and display your jewelry. People can either purchase items at the party, called "cash and carry," or place an order there. Have some refreshments and make the event about socializing, not selling. As a thank-you, gift your host a piece of jewelry. If the party was successful, this will encourage the host to do another one.

Craft Fairs

Craft fairs are a great way to sell your pieces to customers. Every small town and big city has arts and crafts fairs, especially around the holiday season. As an exhibitor, you can network and display your work in a setting where people are already coming to shop for handmade goods. If it is your first time exhibiting at a craft fair, make sure to test your setup beforehand.

WHAT TO CONSIDER BEFORE EXHIBITING AT A CRAFT FAIR

How Much Inventory to Make

When you sign up for a craft show, you have to show up with inventory. While you can bring one set of samples and have people place orders, you will be missing out on tons of sales, as customers become uninterested. It's far better to have lots of merchandise on hand, so craft showgoers can buy what they want right then and take it home.

Unless a piece is one of a kind, start by making two of every piece. When something sells, replace that with two more. Over time you will start to see what your best sellers are and what pieces always sell out at shows.

Added Expenses

Check with the organizer to see if WiFi and electricity are included, or if you need to purchase those. Depending on where the show is, you may consider bringing in extra lights.

You definitely want to be able to accept credit cards. You will almost certainly lose sales if you can't. There are free applications, like Square, that you can download to process credit cards through your smart phone or other mobile devices. You can key in the credit card number, or the company will send you an attachment for your mobile device so you can simply swipe the cards. Check to see if your bank offers a mobile credit card application.

How to Find Out about Craft Fairs

To find out about upcoming events, ask local schools, nonprofit groups, or chambers of commerce about arts and crafts shows you can get involved in. You can also read local newspapers or blogs. Visit websites such as Zapplication.org orCraft-masternews.com for show listings. You can join local, national, or international arts groups, such as the Society of North American Goldsmiths (SNAG), the Enamelist Society, Etsy Street Teams, and Ethical Metalsmith, to learn about shows and gather other information about exhibiting at craft fairs.

CRAFT FAIRS: GETTING THERE AND SETTING UP

Transportation

Keep in mind that you have to get all your jewelry, your booth display, and your packaging materials to the show. Make sure everything fits into the vehicle you are driving and there is still room for passengers. Check with show management about when you can begin unloading and where. If you are by yourself, you most likely won't be able to leave your car unattended, so make sure you look into where you can park your car and how far away it is from the unloading area.

Setup

Store your booth display, marketing materials, and packaging in large plastic bins to make it easy to carry everything to your booth. Bring a small hand truck with you so you can carry all your items in at the same time, and to minimize multiple trips to your car.

If the show is for more than one day, see if there is a secure area where you can store your jewelry. It is never recommended to keep your work out overnight, although a lot of people just drape fabric over their tables. Never leave fine jewelry at your display overnight.

Store extra marketing materials and packaging under your table, so it's easily accessible and you don't need to dig for it.

BOOTH SETUP

TENT

If this is an outdoor fair, consider using a tent in case it rains and to keep your products out of the sun. Many established craft fairs will let you rent one or, if you show at a lot of fairs, you may want to invest in a pop-up tent that is easy to store and transport. Also be prepared for a windy day at an outdoor market. Use something heavy, like sandbags, to keep your table and tent secured. If you have fabric walls on the tent, make sure there are vents cut into them for the wind to blow through. I have had many objects fly away at outdoor markets. Make sure signs and displays are securely tied down as well.

PROPER LIGHTING

This can make or break a show. Without good lighting, your jewelry can get lost. Never assume that a convention hall has good lighting. You have a few seconds to grab customers' attention while they walk by your booth, so make sure they can see what you have on display.

Check with show management about preexisting lighting, and ask if you can bring your own lights. If you just have a table, you can bring some lamps or LED clip-on lights if there is no electricity available. If you are exhibiting underneath a tent, you can most likely rent or bring your own track lighting. You can purchase lighting and bright white halogen lightbulbs from your local hardware store. Also make sure to purchase an adapter, so you can plug it into an electrical socket, as opposed to wiring it into a wall. It's always good to have extra lightbulbs on hand in case one blows out. Consider positioning a mirror to help diffuse the light. Bring zip ties to secure your track on the bars of your tent. Don't forget to bring an extension cord!

While I was exhibiting at a craft fair in a beautiful historic building that featured only natural light from large windows, the space became very dark in the late afternoon into the evening. I made no sales after 4 p.m. because people couldn't see the details and colors in my jewelry. This could have been avoided by contacting show management prior to setup to make sure I was in an area where I could have electricity to add a few lights to my display.

SIGNAGE

Make up a big sign with your company name, logo, and maybe a beautiful picture to display in the center of your booth or to hang off your table. Get a vinyl sign printed at a local print shop or online, which can be transported, displayed, and stored with ease. Get grommets put on your sign—those metal circles on your shower curtain—so you can easily hang it up.

DISPLAY

If you have never exhibited at a craft show before, make sure you practice your setup before you get there. There are two ways you can set up your booth—as an innie or an outie. An innie is where you have your work displayed on the back and side walls inside your booth so the customer can walk in. An outie is where your displays are on the edge of your area so customers look at your work as they walk by. I don't think one setup is better than the other. It depends on what works for you.

TABLES

Bring your own tables or see if you can rent some from the show management. Make sure your tables are heavy and sturdy so they won't blow away at an outdoor show and don't feel flimsy. Cover your tables with long tablecloths so you can discreetly store your empty storage boxes, packaging, and personal items underneath your tables.

Make sure your tables aren't too low. Most people aren't going to bend to pick up your work. Use bed risers to raise your table up so it's closer to eye level.

Jewelry Display

Display your work so it looks clean and reflects your brand. You can purchase necklace, ring, earring, and bracelet forms, or get creative in how you display your items. If you have expensive pieces of jewelry, consider getting a glass jewelry case for your work to put on top of your table. This will make it more difficult for someone to walk off with an item and also make your pieces look like they are more expensive.

Walk craft fairs for ideas on how to exhibit or look at websites like Pinterest for inspiration. Pay attention to displays in retail stores to figure out what works and what doesn't.

Mark Prices Clearly

Most customers want to know how much the item costs so they don't have to ask. Marked prices will also be helpful if you have a friend or assistant step in while you take a break. Be sure to be well versed in pricing to avoid giving different people different information, especially if an admiring customer is returning to make the purchase.

Place stickers, small signs, or hanging price tags directly on pieces. Having the price tag on the actual piece makes less work for you the next time you set up at a show.

Manning the Booth

Make sure you and any helpers know your pricing and materials. Bring a sales order form pad so you can write down what items you sold and give customers a receipt if they pay in cash. If you are using a smartphone application for a credit card processor, it should give you online sales reports and even email or text a receipt to your customer.

Never leave your booth unattended. Unfortunately, there are dishonest people and someone may walk off with your work. It happens all the time. If it's going to be a busy show, ask a friend or family member to join you, or hire an assistant to help so you can each take breaks. It will probably be more fun with a friend anyway!

CRAFT SHOW PACKING LIST

Jewelry

Jewelry display: Neck holders, ring holders, and earring holders—or get creative!

Tablecloth and other booth displays

Signage

Mirror

Packing material (more than you think you need)

Marketing materials: Business cards, postcards, etc.

Notebook for email list signups

Receipt book

Ring sizer

Scissors

Cutting pliers

Price tags

Pens and/or pencils

Calculator

Sandbags (a good idea for an outdoor tent structure)

Polishing cloth

RETAILING ONLINE

Selling your work online can be simple; if you exhibit at craft fairs you will have lots of customers take your information and purchase from your website when they are ready.

Third-Party Websites

List your products on established websites where customers are already looking for handmade items. Etsy, CustomMade, and eBay are all great sites where customers already go to shop.

These platforms are very user-friendly and inexpensive places to list your products. They take care of all the transactions and can even help generate shipping labels. List your products exclusively on one of these sites or on multiple sites and your own website.

Personal e-Commerce Platform

Add a shopping section to your own website so visitors can shop directly from you. This can be an e-commerce platform built into your website, or use sites like BigCartel, Shopify, or Yahoo Small Business for an e-commerce platform.

Post good-quality pictures on white or simple backgrounds with multiple views to show the product clearly. You may also want to feature model shots of the jewelry on a person so the customer can visualize how it would look on them. Read about jewelry photography tips on page 12.

List your product information clearly, including description, materials, dimensions, sizing options, and price. List any variations that are possible and if the item is in stock or is made to order.

Make sure social media sharing options are activated so customers can share your items with their networks and the link will go directly to your site.

WHOLESALE

Wholesale is the selling of a product in large quantities to be resold by other retailers. A retailer is a person who will resell your work at the retail price at a brick-and-mortar shop, through a mail order catalog, or via an online channel. Selling your work in bulk to retailers allows you to focus on what you do best and grow your business on a larger scale. Establishing a wholesale line with new customers and with recurring customers purchasing new designs is the goal for a sustainable business on a larger scale.

Types of Stores

Galleries: Galleries are usually interested in one-of-a-kind pieces, small-scale production, and technical aspects of jewelry making and craft as selling points. Galleries are known to carry high-quality and well-made work, and generally highlight each maker's story. Many galleries purchase work by local artists, buy work from designers who approach them and are a good fit, or find products at trade shows.

Gift and Craft Shops: These stores specialize in high-quality handmade work and mass-produced giftware. Recently, there has been a huge movement to support locally made goods, especially products made in America. Before approaching a gift or craft shop, look at the overall quality of the store's merchandise, the location of the shop, and its reputation. Seek out stores that carry high-quality work. Many gift and craft shops purchase work by local artists, buy work from designers who approach them and are a good fit or buy popular production work they seek out themselves, or find products at trade shows.

Online Stores: Although most brick-and-mortar stores have online shops, a lot of retailers have moved to an online-only presence. Orders for online stores will generally be for multiples of each piece. Have your minimum advertised price (MAP) policy in place so online stores don't undersell your pieces. If you also sell your work in your own online shop, be sure to follow your own MAP policy to avoid conflicts with wholesale accounts. Large online stores will often pull samples to review and photograph with the buying and purchasing teams and then place orders.

Mail Order Catalogs: A handful of catalogs have a great reputation for handmade jewelry. Orders for catalogs will generally be for multiples of each piece. They work quarterly and will always launch their catalog a season ahead. Most catalogs place two initial orders a season—one hard purchase order and one hold for confirmation (HFC) order. An HFC is not a purchase order, but an estimate of what they think they will need to reorder throughout the season. By issuing an HFC, they are asking you to hold onto those products until they issue a purchase order, and then you can ship them. Catalogs will most likely pull samples to review and photograph with the buying and purchasing teams and then place

orders. An account this large with their own warehouse may ask you to provide a UPC, or universal product code, on each item shipped. This is a unique barcode for each SKU that is used for tracking items from shipment, to warehouse, to customer. They will most likely be able to send you the barcodes if you don't have a UPC system in place already.

Department Stores: Most department stores now carry some handmade items. However, since they are bigger than most stores, there are more channels involved in the buying, merchandising, and selling process, and they can be difficult to work with. Some of your smaller customers may be reluctant to work with you if you start selling your work at a large department store, especially if they are discount stores. Department stores will often pull samples to review and photograph with the buying and purchasing teams and then place orders. You may also be asked to send TOP samples, or top-of-production samples, for their quality control department to match your production pieces as they arrive in their warehouse. They generally do not pay for these samples and this is considered the cost of doing business. UPC codes will also likely be used.

Consignment Stores: Consignment is when your products are placed in a store, but you do not get paid until the product sells. In general, consignment merchandise is sold for the wholesale price, but sometimes a percentage is worked out before goods are delivered. Consignment is a terrific way to get your foot in the door at a store where you think your products would sell well, or to break into having your work sold in shops. There are many stores, especially in condensed cities where the competition is high, that sell jewelry only on consignment. This is a terrific way for stores to try out jewelry without having to commit to it and to offer their buyers a wide variety of jewelry. Before agreeing to consign your work, make sure the store has a selection of jewelry that you think your work would do well sitting next to and that the price ranges are similar. Reach out to the other designers to see if they have a good relationship with the consignment store. Both you and the consignment store owner should always sign a consignment agreement specifying in detail which products you're consigning, with each one's wholesale price and suggested retail price, description of materials, responsibility for lost and stolen items, and payment terms (for example: the first of the month). Be mindful when consigning! You are putting a lot of trust in a shop and its employees to represent your pieces well, and also to pay you for items that sell on time. I have a horror story about a store that had thousands of dollars of my merchandise and closed their shop without paying me or returning my items. Unfortunately, this is not the first time I have heard of something like this. Since that happened, I work only with stores that have a good reputation when it comes to consignment with other designers and sell a wide assortment of jewelry. Always go with your gut. I should have gone with mine but was too eager to gain another stockist on my list. It is okay to say no to consigning your work to a store you don't think will represent you well, or where your work doesn't fit in. So be sure you work only with a consignment store that has a good reputation.

Drop-Shipping: Drop-shipping is when an image of your product is listed on a third-party e-commerce website, but the site does not stock the inventory. Instead, when a sale is made, you receive an email and ship the product from your studio. Drop-shipping allows you to get your jewelry listed on a website that has steady traffic and customers who are searching for products like yours. You may work with a wholesaler with a large online presence and only have certain pieces set up to drop-ship. Alternatively, entire websites are set up with a drop-ship model exclusively. Some drop-ship only websites include Designers and Artists and Modalyst. I have worked with wholesalers that stock all my pieces except those that come in different sizes. To avoid stocking too many sizes, these wholesalers have me drop-ship sized items, most commonly rings. Some accounts I've worked with have also made a drop-ship arrangement with me for my more expensive fine jewelry because their warehouse did not have the proper security or insurance for such high-priced items. Another reason to drop-ship is if you have an item that can be customized. Establish

who will be paying for shipping and shipping materials (the e-commerce site should) before entering into a drop-shipping partnership. Establish if the drop-ship website will generate and pay for the shipping label once an order is placed, or if you should create the shipping label and be reimbursed once you are paid for the order. Usually payment is received Net30 to give a window for customer returns.

How to Reach Out to Stores Directly
DO YOUR RESEARCH

Always do your research in advance when approaching a store to carry your jewelry. Check out local stores in your neighborhood

SAMPLE LETTER TO A BUYER

[It's a great idea to find out the name of the appropriate person to send your information to and address the email to her.]

Dear Zoe,

[Use the next paragraph to introduce yourself, your work, and what it entails.]

My name is Emilie Shapiro and I'm the designer and maker of Emilie Shapiro Contemporary Metals [linked to your website]. My jewelry designs are a reflection of nature, celebrating beauty in imperfection. My work features ethically sourced, rough-cut gemstones with recycled brass and sterling silver. I also have a fine-jewelry line using rough diamonds and moonstones cast in place together with 14K yellow gold to represent a marriage of materials.

[Use the following paragraphs to highlight key selling points, like materials, inspiration, and press.]

My work is sold in over fifty stores nationwide, internationally, and online. It has been featured in publications such as *Vogue*, *InStyle*, *Time Out NY*, and more.

Attached are my line sheets for you to review. I would love for you to take a look at my work and to consider carrying it in your store.

You can reply back to this email or give me a call at 555-555-5555 for more information. You can also check out my website at www.emilieshapiro.com.

[Insert an image of your most fabulous piece in the body of this email.]

Thank you,
Emilie

to see what products they carry and if your aesthetic and price points fit in. Begin to make a list of stores you can see your jewelry sold at and what designers you can see your work merchandised next to. Research where else those designers sell and begin to make a wish list of stores. When reaching out to a buyer, make sure it is potentially a good fit and you're getting in touch at the most optimal time.

IN PERSON

Let an employee know you are a local jewelry designer and would love to present your work to the buyer. Make sure you are wearing some of your jewelry; that's the best advertisement! I find that kindness goes a long way. If you are polite and ask for the buyer's information with a smile on your face, most of the time the employee will point you in the right direction.

PHONE AND EMAIL

Reach out to stores you'd like to have carry your work by calling or emailing. When emailing a buyer, keep it short and to the point. Insert an image of your jewelry in the email, and attach line sheets. Sending ten well-thought-out and personalized emails to buyers of stores where you think your work would be a great fit is better than emailing one hundred people with the same copy.

WHOLESALE TRADE SHOWS

The best way to expand your wholesale business is by participating in a trade show. It is a large expense, but there can be a very large return. Trade shows are generally three or four days long and have buyers and press walking the floor searching for new products. Approach a trade show as a marketing expense. The main purpose of a trade show is to build brand awareness and relationships with vendors and create new contacts. It may take time to build these relationships and make sales, so do your research and be persistent.

There are hundreds of fashion, accessory, and gift trade shows in North America and around the world.

Deciding When You Are Ready for a Wholesale Trade Show

Trade shows require a big commitment, so you want to make sure you are ready before you take this major step. It is a good idea to have a few wholesale accounts before attending a show. Many stores like to see that your work is already sold through retail channels before they commit to purchasing from your company. If you feel that you have exhausted all your resources by reaching out to stores in person, via email, and by phone, and can't grow anymore, then it is probably time to consider a wholesale trade show to continue growing.

I highly recommend walking a show to get a feel for other exhibitors and ideas for booth displays, and to see if your work would be a good fit for particular wholesalers (page 120).

What to Expect

At wholesale trade shows, buyers walk the floor to see new collections from existing accounts and search for new designers to pick up. Some buyers will place orders at the show, and some will collect information and place orders afterward. Larger accounts, like department stores, websites, and catalogs, may request samples to review before placing an order.

It is said that someone has to see something seven times before they commit to buying it. This is not always true, of course; I have had buyers who have never before seen my line place an order in thirty seconds. By contrast, I have had buyers look at my line in person twice a year for years before committing. Don't be offended if people aren't knocking down your booth to place orders. Keep in mind that trade shows are marketing and networking expenses. If buyers look at your line and take your information, keep in touch with them. Your jewelry may not be right for them right now, but one day it will be. Some buyers want to see that you are in it for the long haul and will be in business next season. It takes time to establish a brand and carve out your niche in the market. The goal is not just to get sales, but to build relationships with stores, have them reorder throughout the season, and have them be interested in new designs. Always be professional and greet everyone. You never know who anyone is.

Trade show contracts and forms can be very confusing, so don't hesitate to pick up the phone and call someone from the management company or convention center and ask for help.

How to Find the Right Trade Show

There are so many shows to choose from that sometimes it can seem like a daunting task to figure out which one is the right fit for your line. If you are thinking about exhibiting at a show, call the show management, let them know you are interested in applying to exhibit, and ask if you could walk the floor as a guest. Pay attention to the exhibitors and buyers, and see if you can envision your line there. Ask other exhibitors what they think of the show, but be respectful. The exhibitors are there to sell their line, so step aside and let them speak to buyers if someone comes in.

Some trade shows to consider: NY Now, the American Made Show (formerly the Buyers Market of American Craft), ACRE (American Craft Retailers Expo), ENK Accessorie Circuit, D&A (Designer's & Agents) Capsule, COEUR, and ACC (American Craft Council).

Marketing before the Show

Simply setting up a booth at a trade show is not enough to get you noticed. Buyers are flooded with products, so you need to make yourself and your work stand out. There are loads of free and simple ways to promote your work before, during, and after a show so buyers become familiar with your products and want to see more.

MAIL POSTCARDS

Mailing a postcard is a highly effective way to get an image of your work in front of a buyer two to three weeks before a show. Even if you haven't exhibited at that show before, send postcards to the top stores you are hoping to pick up there as clients. Go on the trade show's website to find a list of buyers, so you have an idea of who has attended the show in the past.

Postcards are easy to design with a beautiful image, some information about your brand, trade show details, and contact information. If you don't know how to use design programs like Adobe Photoshop or InDesign, you can find templates through an online printing service. Print postcards on your home computer on thick cardstock or get them printed at a local print shop or online service. Make sure to check what size and resolution your artwork should be before getting your postcards printed. Have postcards on hand at the trade show with your booth number clearly specified. Have the trade show info and booth number printed directly on your postcards, or print labels with that information and adhere them to your postcards so you can use the same postcard for multiple events.

When mailing postcards, check with the post office for the postage cost of the

EMILIE SHAPIRO
CONTEMPORARY METALS

EmilieShapiro.com | 555.555.5555 | sales@EmilieShapiro.com | @EmilieShapiroJewelry

Emilie Shapiro's work is inspired by natural elements and heavily driven by experimentation and process. She incorporates natural, rough gemstones celebrating beauty in imperfections. Emilie uses the ancient craft of lost-wax casting, which dates back to the Egyptians, wherin she carves sculptural pieces into hard wax and casts them into metal. For a primitive yet modern feel, Emilie casts gemstones in place so they are embedded in the metal to represent a marriage of materials.

Emilie uses sustainable business practices by avoiding harsh chemicals in her studio, using recycled metals and packaging materials, and working with vendors who share the same ethos. All jewelry is handmade in Emilie's studio in New York City.

NYNow Handmade I Aug 15–18
Jacob K. Javitz Center
New York City
Booth No. 9183

COEUR I Oct 12–14
Alexandria Ballroom, Mezz Level
Los Angeles

EmilieShapiro.com I 555.555.5555 I sales@EmilieShapiro.com I @EmilieShapiroJewelry

size postcard you are sending. Be sure to use the appropriate stamp to avoid getting them returned back to you.

EMAIL MARKETING

Email marketing is an effective way to stay in touch with customers and build a relationship. Have an email list exclusively for wholesale customers. Send email blasts out with your upcoming trade show schedule with images of your new designs and any exciting news you're looking to share. Be sure to link the trade show registration website in your email with dates, location, and your booth number. It's a great idea to let buyers know they can make an appointment with you at the trade show to guarantee they will meet the designer. Also note that if they are not attending the show they should respond back to the email to receive updated line sheets. Read more about email marketing on page 101.

SOCIAL MEDIA

Social media is an extremely effective way to market your pieces before, during, and after a trade show. Many people, including the top buyers of stores and boutiques, look to social media for inspiration and to help navigate events because it is so accessible. Post images of your work using Instagram, Facebook, Twitter, and Tumblr, and tag the show's social media handle.

Use the show's designated hashtag to make it easy for buyers and press to find out about your brand. When stores place orders, ask if they use social media and post a picture on their social media networks of a piece they purchased from you. They may repost it, which is a terrific way for you to cross promote each other's business. When I ship orders out to wholesale accounts, I like to post a taste of what they're getting and tag their social media account. I generally find that buyers appreciate you promoting your work that's sold at their store and it gets them excited about what's coming. Read more about social media on page 102.

FREE MARKETING TOOLS FROM THE TRADE SHOW

Check with the trade show management about free marketing tools that are available to you. Inquire if there is an area for press kits. A press kit is a packet consisting of a company overview, a designer biography, photos of your work, and frequently asked questions. If you have received press coverage, include one or two of the most recent clippings or the largest coverage you have received.

At NY Now, the largest trade show where I exhibit twice a year, a juried section is designated for "Made in America" and "Sustainability" products that are showcased to buyers when they enter the convention center. This is a free way to get your products in front of buyers and press and entice them to come to your booth. Check in with show management for other free marketing tools they have available.

Display

Create a display that highlights your jewelry and your overall aesthetic but does not compete with your work. Most trade show booths come as a blank canvas with gray carpet, pipe and drape, and a chair. Pipe and drape is a freestanding system to block off your area with a standard black or white curtain hanging from the sides to give the illusion of walls. You can bring your own furniture and display, or rent these from the trade show company. Prop companies also rent out furniture for trade shows and may have a more interesting selection than the trade show's recommended company. Renting from one of these companies is usually very pricey but may be worthwhile if

you are traveling from out of town. Most big box furniture companies have at least one store in major cities if you need standard-size shelves or tables. It will most likely cost you less money to purchase these items when you arrive than it will to rent them. If you travel for shows a lot, you can also consider renting a storage unit in the city for your display to avoid shipping it across the country multiple times a year. There are companies who specialize in trade show shipping and storing. Look for these on the trade show website or ask management who they represent. When you register for a trade show, you will most likely get many solicitation phone calls and emails from companies like these.

LIGHTING

Lighting is extremely important at a trade show and can enhance or detract from your display. Convention centers often have strict rules on hanging your own lights, so make sure to inquire and read the contracts thoroughly. You can save a lot of money at a trade show by bringing your own track lighting. You can find track lighting at any large hardware store and attach these lights with zip ties to the pipe and drape. Make sure to purchase the adapter that connects into the track, so you can plug the lights into an electrical socket. Buy bright white lights and always have extra lightbulbs on hand. It is a good idea to purchase more lights than you think you need. Once your booth is set up, you can direct the lights at your jewelry to make sure it is all well lit. Don't forget to also point lights on your signage on the walls. Avoid creating shadows on your pieces by having lots of light.

You can also rent lights from the trade show company and have them installed by the convention center's electrical team. This is a great option if you are traveling for the show and have limited space for the items you are bringing. Be prepared to spend a few hundred dollars to rent lights. Don't forget to purchase electricity if it is not included. Usually it is not.

At the first trade show where I ever exhibited, I used warm-colored flood lightbulbs in clamp lights. My work looked horrible and the lights looked messy! Although I learned from my mistakes, I wasted a lot of money and lost many potential sales at that first show because I didn't do enough research or ask for help.

WALL COVERINGS

You can transform your whole space by changing the wall color. Use inexpensive curtains or fabric to hang from the pipes. Keep in mind when purchasing fabric that most convention centers require you to use flame-retardant fibers as a safety measure. Read more about flame-retardant fibers at the end of this section. Adhere grommets, the metal circles often found on shower curtains, to your fabric and attach it to the pipes using large 4-inch (10-cm) S-hooks. You can find these materials at your local hardware store or purchase them online. Another option is to attach to your fabric a piece of wood with eye hooks screwed in. I use this option because I find it easy to hang up quickly, and the fabric looks a little smoother. Use 1-inch-by-1-inch (2.5 cm x 2.5 cm) pieces of wood cut into 2-foot (61-cm) sections. Staple-gun the fabric to the back of the wood, and place eye hooks on either end of the wood. Use 4-inch (10-cm) S-hooks to connect the eye hooks to the pipe and drape. I like doing this in 2-foot (61-cm) sections so I have many options, depending on the size of my booth at each show.

You can also use a heavy-duty fire-retardant paper to cover the walls for a nice, seamless look that feels a little bit more like a solid wall. You can purchase this paper in any color and any size. Make sure to check the height of your pipe and drape—it's usually 8 feet (2.4 m) high—and the length you will need to cover all your walls. To attach the paper to the pipes, use 8-inch (20.5-cm) spring clamps that you can purchase in the electrical section of any large hardware store.

Another way to create a seamless look in your booth is to put up hard walls. Depending on your package, some trade shows include a hard wall booth. You may be able to rent a hard wall display from the trade show company, but this will be a very expensive option. You can build your own hard walls by building a frame, and then attaching a wood board to the front. Paint your wood with a fire-retardant paint available at a home improvement store. Line up the wood panels in your booth with the frame facing the back, and attach them to each other using spring clamps or another temporary method that is easy to assemble and disassemble. You may want to bring a small container of the paint and a brush for touchups as needed.

Keep in mind that most exhibition centers do not allow you to use power tools, so your booth structure should be as easy to take apart and put together as possible. Build your frames before you get to the show, so all you have to do is clamp them together.

To create a faux hard wall look, use large poster board panels and adhere them together by drilling holes 1 inch (2.5 cm) from the edge of each board and use a clear zip tie to attach them from behind. You can generally find poster board panels in white, but you can paint them, stick wallpaper on them, or even place custom logo designs on them. You can order 8-foot- (2.4-m) high poster boards online and get them shipped right to the convention center.

Most convention centers have rules in place about the use of flammable materials, so make sure you understand those rules to avoid incurring penalties. Sometimes using natural fibers instead of synthetic ones is enough to meet the fire-safety regulations. Instead of purchasing expensive flameproof fabric from the trade show company's recommended vendor, you can purchase a flameproofing kit. You usually spray the solution on or put it in a washing machine with your fabric. You can make your own flameproofing solution using 7 parts borax, 3 parts boric acid, and 100 parts water. Dip your fabric in this solution and let it dry. If you have wood displays, you can purchase flameproof paint at any large hardware store.

FLOOR COVERINGS

Some convention centers have rules that you must cover your own floor, so make sure to inquire about this and read the contract thoroughly. This is also an easy way to customize and brighten up your booth by bringing in a faux hardwood floor or a fun area rug. Consider getting a padded floor that will be easy on your feet, especially since you'll be standing most of the day. Flooring companies sell 2-foot-by-2-foot (61 cm x 61 cm) interlocking square carpet or foam flooring. These are great because they enable you to change the configuration of your floor, depending on the dimensions of your booth. If you are putting down a rug, get an inexpensive non-slip mat to place underneath it. You do not want you or anyone else tripping on your floor covering. Find flooring at many big box retailers or online stores. If you don't need to have your floors covered, you may consider asking the trade show company for no carpet (if it's included) to leave the concrete floor exposed for an industrial look.

SIGNAGE AND PHOTOGRAPHS

When designing your booth, keep in mind that it takes buyers about two seconds to walk by your booth, and they will be looking from a side angle, not straight on. So a wonderful way to showcase your designs is through large photographs on the walls of your booth. These grab buyers' attention as they are walking by.

I like to use vinyl signs with photographs of my top-selling pieces and some shots of me working in the studio to show the pieces being made by hand. Vinyl is ideal because you do not have to worry about the signs wrinkling, like fabric, or tearing, like paper. You can get these signs printed at your local printing store or you can order them online from a printing service. You can get grommets on the corners so you can hang the signs from S-hooks on the pipe. Don't forget to include a booth sign with your company logo and booth number clearly printed to avoid confusion. If you don't have your booth number on your sign, I guarantee you will have buyers looking all around your booth for it.

DESIGNING YOUR DISPLAY

When designing your display, try to build an environment that is aligned with the stores that will carry your jewelry. Be careful not to make your display overpower your jewelry. Keeping it simple is always best.

My work is organic, earthy, and uses rough gemstones, so I use three-tiered wooden display tables to create different levels, with white jewelry forms for a fresh and natural feeling. I incorporate props like green air plants, driftwood, and shells to exude an organic feel and show where my inspiration comes from. If your work is more architectural, try clean lines and contrasting colors and textures. Opt for no carpet in your booth and utilize the industrial look of the concrete floor. Try to make your space feel like a retail store that reflects your style.

Since your real estate at a trade show is very expensive, try to maximize your space by building up. If you are using tables, consider making two or three tiers and having your lowest display close to eye level. You can make or purchase risers for added height, or use interesting props for elevation.

If you have the room for it, you may want to include a small table to write orders on and a chair or two. Buyers will definitely appreciate a place to sit, and it will probably keep them there longer, too! If you don't have room for this, bring a few clipboards so you can write the orders while standing.

If you are exhibiting fine jewelry, consider putting it in a jewelry case. It makes the work appear to be more expensive and is most likely how buyers merchandise fine jewelry in their stores.

MERCHANDISING

Present your jewelry in a clean and cohesive way. Don't overcrowd your display; otherwise, you'll overwhelm buyers with too many choices. If you have many color options for the same piece, consider putting your best-selling choice out and keeping the other options on a tray so you can show buyers if they are interested.

Clearly label all your wholesale prices on or next to your pieces. This way, buyers don't have to keep asking you how much something is, and they will appreciate it. I like to use a clear jewelry tag on every individual piece to avoid any confusion if the pieces get moved around. This will also be helpful if you have someone assisting you and your assistant doesn't know all the prices off the top of her head.

Getting There and Setting Up

If you are traveling to exhibit at the trade show, you may need to ship your display and supplies to the convention center. If you are flying, think about what large items you can rent, like tables and display cases, and what you can carry on the plane, like jewelry and small supplies. If you need to ship items to the convention center, you can use FedEx or UPS and designate your package(s) to arrive directly at the convention center and be placed in your booth area. There are also shipping companies that cater to trade shows that you can use. Once you register for a trade show, most likely you will get loads of solicitation calls from these shipping companies.

If you travel to the same city for trade shows a few times a year, consider keeping your display in a local storage unit. It may be less expensive to pay the monthly rent for a storage unit than to ship your booth display back and forth.

If you are driving to the show, check with show management about when you can begin setting up and where you offload your display. Make sure your whole display and passengers can fit in whatever vehicle you're driving to the show. Dress comfortably and in layers for setup day; convention centers can be steaming hot and freezing all in a day. Bring a hand truck to load your display to bring to your booth. Some shows have free porter service available, so definitely check with show management to take advantage of that. Pack your display in plastic bins that are easy to stack, transport, and store. You may want to bring a stepladder to easily hang wall coverings and signs.

If you have empty cartons from shipping, the convention center will store them for you. When you break down at a trade show, sometimes it can take hours to get your empty cartons back. If you shipped your items, you don't have a way of getting around this. If you are hand-carrying your items, condense your cartons as best as you can. You may find a spot in your display to tuck them away so no one sees them.

Manning the Booth

Dress the part! Not only are you representing your jewelry, but you are projecting an image of your business and your brand, too. Wear nice clothes in the style of your jewelry, and, of course, wear all your best-selling pieces. A high-end gallery may be deterred if you are wearing leggings and a T-shirt.

You should be standing and greeting people who come by, not sitting and looking preoccupied by something else. An exhibitor who's texting is sure to lose some customers. These are long days, but you will look much more approachable when you are standing with a smile on your face. Greet everyone who walks by, but let each of them digest what is in front of them before you start your sales pitch. Buyers like to have a few moments to take in the work and consider if they can see it in their store before you give them your sales pitch. Engage in a conversation, but don't rush to tell them why they should buy your products. Most buyers find that annoying, it makes them feel awkward, and they will be turned off.

If they are looking at a piece that is out

of their reach, hand it to them. Most of the time, buyers stick around longer when they are physically touching your work. People often feel they can't touch the work on display, so be approachable and make them feel comfortable. Consider bringing an assistant to help you, even if it is only for a few hours a day so you can go to the bathroom, eat lunch, and walk around a little. Make sure to educate your assistant about your work, your materials, and how to take an order. If you don't know someone who can assist you, ask show management to recommend someone.

Making a Sale

Certain stores will place an order, sometimes referred to as writing an order, at the show. When I start to write an order, I immediately ask for the buyer's business card so I can begin filling out his information on the purchase order form, and ask him if the billing and shipping addresses are the same as on his card. While I am filling out his contact information, I give the buyer a jewelry tray with items he's considering buying, so he can select the merchandise for his order. I like to snap a photo of the tray on my smartphone when the buyer is done choosing the pieces he wants, in case I

overlooked something when I was writing the order.

Unless it is an established account, I require a credit card to take the order. If buyers are reticent about giving you a credit card, let them know they can use another card when you run the balance. Don't feel shy about asking a buyer for a credit card. It is industry standard to require a credit card to process an order, so don't let anyone bully you into taking an order without one. The majority of the accounts I have had payment issues with have been those whose buyers refused to give me a credit card when placing the order. If you act professionally and project an aura that you know exactly what you're talking about, no one will know it's your first trade show and you are freaking out internally that you just got your first order!

I require new accounts to pay the full balance before the order is shipped, but existing accounts can establish terms that work for them. Establish payment terms that you are comfortable with and state them clearly on your purchase order form and line sheets to avoid confusion. Write the SKU and quantity first to make sure the most important information is recorded. I fill in the rest of the product information from the SKU on the purchase order later, if I don't have time to do this at the sale, especially when buyers are in a rush.

Networking

Keep in mind that trade shows are a networking expense. Dedicate a notebook to keep track of your contacts. Gaining contacts is one of the most important parts of a trade show. Not every store will commit to an order right away. Buyers may want to watch you grow and evolve. Keep in touch with your new contacts, and they will turn into clients.

After you meet someone, staple her business card to a page in your book or write down her contact information in the book. Write down what you spoke about and what pieces she was interested in. The days at a trade show are long, and you will be talking to hundreds of people; most likely you will forget most of these conversations by the end of the day. A notebook is a great way to keep track of all your new contacts and remember what you spoke about.

Follow up with everyone you meet at the show via email. Customize your follow-up emails with images of the pieces buyers were interested in, reference what

you spoke about, and attach your line sheets. I like to do this the night I meet them and then again a few weeks after the show. Don't forget to include ordering information and your booth number in case they come back to the show the next day.

Following up with store buyers is extremely important. You can't rely on buyers to remember you and reach out to you after a show to place an order. Make it a priority to follow up with past, current, and potential customers quarterly. Pick up the phone or send them an email to check in on the work they currently have and see if they have any questions, or tell them about new pieces. If you feel shy about making sales calls, write yourself a script so you make sure to touch on all the points you want to cover. The goal in business is to build long-term relationships with customers. If you follow up with your accounts via email and phone, they will know that you are easy to do business with and great at communicating.

Breaking Down

Breaking down from a trade show can be absolutely insane. Everyone is exhausted and wants to go home. Don't be lazy. Pack your jewelry and display neatly, so the next time you open the boxes up everything is intact and not damaged during transport. If you stored your empty cartons, sometimes it can take a few hours to get them back. Convention center employees start breaking down the show about thirty seconds after it ends, so try to stay calm in the chaos and pay attention so you don't get hurt.

TRADE SHOW PACKING LIST

Jewelry

Jewelry display: Neck forms, earring forms, ring forms

Booth display: Tables, shelves, wall coverings, floor covering, signs, chairs, props

Price tags

Office supplies: Pens and pencils, stapler, correction fluid, superstrong glue, calculator

Purchase order forms

Jewelry trays (for buyers to spread out orders on)

Clipboards (to write on while taking orders)

Notebook for business cards and contacts

Line sheets (50 printed copies)

Postcards and/or business cards with your booth number

Jewelry emergency kit: Polishing cloth, pliers, earring backs, clear fishing line

Clear zip ties, 4-inch (10-cm) S-hooks, 8-inch (20.5-cm) spring clamps, binder clips

Track lighting with adapter to plug into electrical socket

Extension cord(s)

Multiplug outlet

Lights with extra lightbulbs

Stepladder

Water and snacks: Nobody likes a grumpy exhibitor! Stay hydrated and bring some snacks in case you don't have time to run out for lunch.

SALES REPS AND SHOWROOMS

Why to Work with a Sales Rep or Showroom

Handling your own sales is certainly not for everyone. When selling your work, you need to be able to speak about your pieces, materials, and inspirations and tell store buyers what the main selling points are. Buyers want to know why their customers are going to want to purchase this work. It is hard for some artists and designers to detach themselves from the creative process and communicate the selling points of their jewelry. You may choose to work with a sales representative or a showroom if you don't like handling sales and want to focus on other aspects of the business, or if you begin to have a lot of wholesale accounts and need help keeping up with sales and gaining more exposure. You can hire an in-house sales rep or an independent sales rep, or work with a showroom. Whichever way you decide to go, make sure your sales rep or showroom is passionate about your work and represents other like-minded brands.

Sales representatives take your jewelry to stores where they have relationships and show it in person. They will usually travel to a store a few times a year with a set of samples for a sales meeting. Sales reps generally represent a few different lines and often have a territory, like the tristate New York metropolitan area (New York, New Jersey, and Connecticut), that they cover and where they have strong business relationships.

Showrooms are a dedicated space where brands have permanent representation. Buyers come to showrooms specifically to see what products are on display and to work with sales reps there. Pick a showroom that has a good reputation and carries work similar to yours. Showrooms will most likely have one or a few booths at trade shows. This is a great place to see the other work they carry and speak with

a sales rep. Showrooms also cover territories; if they are large, they generally have a showroom in major cities. Major US cities with large showrooms, like New York City, Atlanta, Las Vegas, Dallas, Los Angeles, and Chicago, are also centers for international trade shows. Showroom managers often reach out to you if they would like to work with you.

Before deciding to work with a sales representative or a showroom, consider the expense it will add to your overhead. Sales reps generally take a 10–15 percent commission off a wholesale order, but I have heard of commissions running as high as 25 percent. When working with a showroom, you also pay rent on top of the commission, anywhere from $500 to $1,000 a month. Also consider the time and expense involved in making an additional set of jewelry samples for each rep. If you already know you're planning to work with reps and showrooms, take these expenses into consideration when pricing your jewelry.

How to Find the Right Person

Finding a good and dedicated sales representative can be difficult. You need someone who is passionate and knowledgeable about your work, and represents other brands that complement yours but don't compete. You don't want the stores they are pitching to to purchase items from another one of their lines instead of yours. You also don't want the other lines they represent to be so completely different from yours that they appeal to a different type of store altogether.

Reps will often reach out to you if they are interested in representing you. An effective way to find a sales rep is to ask the stores you already work with if they can make any recommendations. You can also look for classified ads in the back of craft magazines like *Metalsmith Magazine*, *Niche*, *Giftware News*, and the like. Reps will often walk trade shows to seek out new brands as well.

If you don't like doing all the legwork to get new sales and maintain those accounts, contracting with one or more sales reps can be a great idea. Sales reps can help grow your business by representing your line in their territories and can cover more ground than you could alone.

On the other hand, you may like handling sales. I love connecting with buyers. They love to meet the artist and hear me talk about my inspirations and passions. When I am present at a trade show or event, I sell much more than

when someone else is representing my work. You need to find what works for you and your work.

SOME FINAL TIPS FOR SUCCESS

Make Your Own Decisions— You're the Boss!

Whether you're hiring an employee, deciding if a new store is a good (or a bad) fit for your work, or telling the owner of a store he can't change your designs, you'll make scads of big decisions when you're running a craft business. You are the designer and the boss!

As an artist, you have a tendency to make decisions based on feelings and intuition. As a successful businessperson, you need to make decisions based on rational calculation. I like to strike a happy medium between the two.

When you need help, ask for it. Use the resources of friends, family, and local businesses around you. No one can do everything!

Be Thoroughly Professional

Accept nothing less than the highest standards for your work. Never cut corners to make a deadline; your work will suffer and people will notice. Customers buy handmade because these are good-quality products. The goodwill of your customers is your most valuable asset! Don't jeopardize it by delivering late or shipping work that's not top quality.

Never stop learning!

There is always more to learn about this business. Continue to experiment with your craft by taking classes, attending trade shows, and researching what others in the industry are up to. Trust me, it's worth it!

Insider Guidance from Industry Professionals

✦

QUESTIONS FOR BUYERS AND DESIGNERS

How do designers pitch new designs to you?

"Every object has a story and I enjoy exploring and understanding the narrative as much as the object itself. As an artist, I respond to a designer's passion for their process as much as what they create. Their enthusiasm ignites my own. I work closely with designers to curate products along relevant seasonal story lines. When a designer approaches me with new work, we discuss how it builds on their existing portfolio and how that forms part of a cohesive selection that complements what we have in stock."

—Jenah Barry, Owner, Xylem & Phloem

"Either through email, at a trade show, or by making an appointment with us at our office or their showroom."

—Erin Fergusson, Director of Merchandising, Rodale's

"I am always open and excited to see something new. Due to limited hours in the day, usually first impressions are made through pictures via email. That is the best way for me to get a read whether the line is brand appropriate off the bat before too much time is invested by either party."

—Ashleigh Bergman, Senior Buyer for Jewelry, Anthropologie

"It's wonderful when existing partners send info on new seasonal capsules—often as buyers we forget to wrap around with

137

designers we have worked with in the past. As far as blind submissions go, those are usually filtered through a corporate email address and not always the most efficient way to get in contact with the buying team."

—Julie Malone, Associate Buyer for Kitchen and Garden, Rodale's

"Usually I will go to different trade shows and design hives to seek new talent. Some designers will pitch ideas via: email (sending me line sheets); call (letting me know that they have new styles). Instagram is also a way designers will pitch ideas—and where I find new talent. Less formal, but I think more effective."

—Silvana Costa, Buyer and Owner, The Wicked Peacock

"Designers pitch their designs in a variety of ways. First, we have a new goods submission portal that allows designers to forward their work directly to us, and a buyer will look at each and every submission. If the piece or collection seems like it may be a good addition to our assortment, we will request a sample and show it to our team in our weekly sample meeting. We also attend numerous trade shows, craft fairs, and maker markets throughout the year—we scout for new designers that may be right for us, and

work with existing designers on new ideas. All the buyers on our team also are active in seeing what's out there in the marketplace via online research. We are constantly scouting and will reach out directly to designers who seem like a good fit to work with us. We'll then work with that designer to put together a sample pack for us so we can see their work in person."

—Sharon Hitchcock, Senior Buyer, UncommonGoods

"We get a lot of direct mail, email, and sometimes even phone calls. I prefer email and mailers to phone calls; you can't see what the aesthetic and brand is from a cold call. But the most important (and valuable) way we find new designers is through our Open Call, a quarterly program for NYC-based talent."

—Camilla Gale, Buyer and Owner, Thistle & Clover

"Most designers will send an email. Some emails include line sheets or look books. I personally find look books more valuable when discovering a new-to-me brand. It helps to get a sense of the vibe and the target customer. It always makes an even bigger impression when designers send me physical copies of the look book in the mail. Very few people do that anymore, and when I do receive them, they never go straight to the trash, as is the case with a lot of emails."

—Victoria Chiodo,
Retail Gallerist, Darioush

What stands out to you in a pitch? What are some mistakes you see in pitches?

"I always look for someone who truly believes in their product. There are no rules; be true to yourself. I respond to creative and friendly approaches—rather than pushy pitches; after all a pitch is about tone. This means listening carefully to questions about your process and work and responding to the questions in a focused manner. So have your responses ready, but ultimately make sure you understand what you are actually being asked and consider your response. Subtlety aside, it is so important to clearly articulate in simple terms what you are selling (jewelry/necklaces), the materials (silver/fiber), the price point, and its general look/inspiration (botanical/organic minimalist). It's also important to connect it to the mission/philosophy of the store/entity it is entering—motivate why it is a great fit for this particular retail avenue. Remember that buyers are going to be reselling your product to their clients—so make it easy

for people selling your product to get to know it and be comfortable fielding questions from customers. How would you describe your product in a couple of lines both clearly and sensually? What is it that makes it stand out?"

—Jenah Barry, Owner, Xylem & Phloem

"People who actually research your business and understand your brand requirements! They are better at tailoring their pitch to highlight why their product is a fit for your business. People that have no idea what your business is about often make the biggest mistakes or shouldn't have pitched to you in the first place. Not providing the full story behind a product and why it is special is also a common misstep. As retailers, we often ask ourselves if the price/value relationship of a product is strong before we decide to sell the product. For more expensive products, it helps tremendously if the person pitches the product with information about the quality of the materials, the quality of the craftsmanship, etc., to help answer that price/value question."

—Erin Fergusson, Director
of Merchandising, Rodale's

"For me, it is ALL about product. Yes, the 'story' is also important, but I think too many words could be a mistake. So great photography is key, along with clear messaging on product content and price. If the pitch is at a trade show, having a creative booth always draws people in. If the pitch is in an office, keep it simple and clean. Make the product display easy and approachable so the buyer won't be afraid to touch and/or try on."

—ASHLEIGH BERGMAN, SENIOR BUYER
FOR JEWELRY, ANTHROPOLOGIE

"The work has to speak for itself— everything else isn't as important. Margins need to be realistic (e.g., some companies only need 55 percent, but my former company required a 75 percent margin!) so that the buyers aren't put in a pinch when they love the product but can't work it into their buying plan. Mistakes are when designers are pushy, or try to convince you that they know your customer better than you do, or try to TALK YOU INTO buying the product. If it doesn't come naturally, it isn't meant to be."

—JULIE MALONE, ASSOCIATE BUYER
FOR KITCHEN AND GARDEN, RODALE'S

"It's all about the work. I am a very particular buyer, and I know my customers very well. I'm not the kind of buyer who is 'sold' on something with pitches like,

'this is my best-selling piece' and 'all my boutiques order this piece.'"

—SILVANA COSTA, BUYER AND OWNER,
THE WICKED PEACOCK

"Preparation is key! I know it may sound simplistic, but being prepared makes a world of difference. As a buyer, I see a large volume of submissions. Having information to make an informed decision is so important—pricing, materials, inspiration, lead time, capacity—these are all questions that a designer should be prepared to answer.

One of the biggest mistakes I come across is a designer's pricing structure. Many designers are used to selling their collection at retail shows, craft fairs, through their own website, or a third-party retail platform. There can be difficulty in pricing their goods within a wholesale pricing structure. It's about figuring out not only material costs, but other things such as paying yourself fairly for your time. I think the first thing a designer should evaluate is if it's possible to wholesale their designs. Is it realistic with their current business structure? Wholesale isn't right for everyone and that's OK! A designer should really crunch the numbers and see if selling wholesale is a workable arrangement and makes financial sense. The other question a designer should ask themselves is if it's possible to scale their business if a larger account is interested. That will help inform their decisions about how/where to market to retailers. Do they want to start offering their collection to smaller boutiques or are they prepared to go after larger retailers? Before a designer pitches an item, wholesale pricing structure should be resolved."

—Sharon Hitchcock, Senior Buyer,
UncommonGoods

"A good pitch is from someone who is personable, visibly passionate about their line and trade, organized, open-minded, and understands both the boutique's brand and their own. Our Open Call is about dialogue as much as it is about selling; it's imperative that new designers are willing to take constructive criticism from buyers no matter whether it's concerning aesthetic, customer base, workmanship, or price point."

—Camilla Gale, Buyer and Owner,
Thistle & Clover

"I can tell when designers have done their research on my store and have selected it as a good fit for their collection. Many of the lines I see are nice but just not a fit for my store, and it's clear that the designer hasn't done her research or targeted my store specifically. I think it's ultimately a better use of your time and the buyer's time if you focus on pitching to the right stores as opposed to as many stores as possible. Plus, it's not just about who will pay you for your work, but who do you want to align yourself with as a brand."

—Victoria Chiodo,
Retail Gallerist, Darioush

What is your buying process/ schedule like?

"It's seasonal. I usually place orders three months in advance—placing orders in winter for spring and summer and in summer for fall and winter. I also look for designs that speak to the season but are enduring year-round—New York is tangibly different in spring, summer, fall, and winter. While I often order well in advance and appreciate lead times on handcrafted designs, I do like to receive products within a month of the order being placed."

—Jenah Barry, Owner, Xylem & Phloem

"We set a seasonal merchandising strategy about six months prior to the season we are planning. We set the category plans (which categories are growing or shrinking), we set merchandising themes that we need to assort to (for example, for fall we have an apple harvest theme), and we land on a ballpark number of items we are looking for within each category and theme. For apparel, we follow the standard apparel market calendar for buying. As with most online retailers, market goods in the other categories are discovered, approved, and set live on our site on a rolling basis. We obviously prioritize the most important products depending on what is selling, what is on trend, etc."

—Erin Fergusson, Director
of Merchandising, Rodale's

"In terms of schedule, we are constantly reviewing product. If it is 'a love,' I will always find a place for it. The process usually starts with me finding designers through trade shows, Internet research, traveling, and stopping people on the street to ask what they are wearing. I also get a lot of inspiration from vintage jewelry, which I then will have developed into something unique. Additionally I get tons of emails and sample submissions from new designers. Then if I am interested in the lines, I will request specific product off the line sheets. We go through product every few days and put aside pieces that fit into the looks/stories/silhouettes we

are going after that season. If we love something but it isn't seasonally appropriate, we store it in our huge sample archives for later consideration. We get multiple rounds of feedback from our cross functional partners such as the visual team, store teams, merchandising, and marketing, as well as our GMM, CMO, and sometimes CEO before we land on the buy."

—Ashleigh Bergman, Senior Buyer
for Jewelry, Anthropologie

"We build seasonal capsules around trends and themes we feel are important and then create collections from designers around that. We go to market a few times a year to glean these trends as well as make new collections."

—Julie Malone, Associate Buyer
for Kitchen and Garden, Rodale's

"I do major travel in the winter (Jan/ Feb) to buy for the store. I will usually hit three to five trade shows in this time across the USA. I am the kind of buyer who makes small, frequent buys and it is a successful strategy for me. When I bring in a new designer line, I am cautious and really don't want to invest more than $500 initially."

—Silvana Costa, Buyer and Owner,
The Wicked Peacock

"We are a catalog and web business, and we are always working several months ahead of our catalog mailings for items with potential catalog placement. For web-only items, we are always reviewing products and have weekly sample meetings to review new designs, and approve on a rolling basis as SKU availability and budgets allow."

—Sharon Hitchcock, Senior Buyer, UncommonGoods

"For clothing, we buy according to market, i.e., we buy spring clothing in September and fall clothing in February with capsule collections showing shortly thereafter. For jewelry and accessories, we have no set schedule except for our quarterly Open Call."

—Camilla Gale, Buyer and Owner, Thistle & Clover

"As much as possible, I like to plan out my seasons in advance, but that usually amounts to well-planned large buys and a general sketch of the vibe for the season. I definitely buy on an ongoing basis and love discovering something mid-season and picking it up right away with a smaller buy. That said, it's a bummer when designers can't accommodate immediate or between-season orders. I

definitely understand the importance of preordering collections, but I appreciate a little flexibility on the part of the designer because if I'm excited about something new, I usually want it right away!"

—Victoria Chiodo, Retail Gallerist, Darioush

What do you look at when looking at jewelry samples?

"Quality and materials—trade-relevant material specifications, workmanship, stone cut, patina, karat, settings. Also, a tactile and sensual quality—how does it look and feel? Fit and function. The beauty of individual pieces. The cohesiveness of a collection. The availability of a range of price points from high (statement pieces) to low (affordable smaller pieces) is a big factor."

—Jenah Barry, Owner, Xylem & Phloem

"Material quality, general feel of the piece (substantial or flimsy?), comfort of fit, if the item will photograph well."

—Erin Fergusson, Director of Merchandising, Rodale's

"There is a great deal to consider when looking at samples. There is always the initial reaction and gut/emotional response. Then you consider quality of materials and construction, is it on-brand, is it bringing something fresh that you haven't offered before, will it surprise and delight her, is it versatile and easy to wear, will it draw her to the fixture or is it more of a key item, does it have hanger appeal or would it be a better fit to be shot solely for the web, is it something she won't be able to find anywhere else, will she appreciate the price/value relationship?"

—Ashleigh Bergman, Senior Buyer
for Jewelry, Anthropologie

"Quality. Is it fussy? Fit."

—Julie Malone, Associate Buyer
for Kitchen and Garden, Rodale's

"Style, quality, price, how it will display in my store. I see a lot of 'indy' designer work that sells at too high of a price point for the quality of the metals—in my opinion."

—Silvana Costa, Buyer and Owner,
The Wicked Peacock

"I am always looking for a particular aesthetic that I believe will appeal to our customer. Sometimes it's more obvious, and sometimes it's a direction we are nudging them toward. I also look at craftsmanship. I love to see something quirky that makes a piece or collection a little different than others I've seen.

It might be an unusual material or technique, it might be an innovative setting, or it might be something with a sly sense of humor. Something that has a little spark and makes your heart feel happy when you see it—that is what sets a piece or collection apart. I also am very interested in the story of how the designer came to do what he or she does. I am fascinated by the different ways that people come to the world of jewelry design. I work with designers who've had years of formal training, others who are completely self-taught, and all sorts of situations in between. The common thread that I hear over and over from our designers is how they can't really imagine doing anything else. They have such a love for their craft."

—Sharon Hitchcock, Senior Buyer,
UncommonGoods

"I look at workmanship and an overall presentation. Is the collection cohesive? Does it have a core group of styles that stay consistent season after season? It's important for jewelry designers to know that you don't have to always reinvent the wheel. We have been selling some of the same styles from veteran jewelry designers at T&C since we opened in 2008. I also look at price point and what kind of metals the designer is using. Are those prices going to be viable in our market? If they are big-ticket items, do they check any specialty boxes like engagement and wedding? I can usually tell if I'll be able to go forward with an order within the first couple minutes of seeing the line."

—Camilla Gale, Buyer and Owner,
Thistle & Clover

"Jewelry buying can be difficult simply because a lot of it looks the same these days. I look for collections that have something new to say, either with the aesthetic or the materials (recycles, hand cut, uncommon materials, etc). I also look for a range of price points. I know that the majority of the pieces I buy are going to fall within a certain range, but I also want that knockout inspiration piece that will anchor my display and also help sell the other pieces.

A point of personal frustration: I understand that most designs can be made with different metals or stones, but telling me verbally about all the options is very overwhelming. I'm very visual and I need to see it. At the very least, show the completed design and have an assortment of all the raw stones for me to see. And remember that you are the designer, not me. I don't need to 'build my own' jewelry

line. Feel confident letting your designs stand on their own; I probably don't want as many options as you might think I do."

—Victoria Chiodo,
Retail Gallerist, Darioush

Any dos and don'ts for wholesale trade shows?

"Do: Ideally the product should sell itself with the right combination of quality and pricing. Ahead of the show, cultivate your relationship with past and current buyers . . . Buyers receive a lot of mass mailings of postcards and catalogs ahead of shows, so make yours special but practical. A handwritten note, warm personal message, or product sample is always appreciated. At the show: Say hello, smile, make eye contact, be friendly and approachable (rather than hovering at the entrance to your booth, blocking the entrance, in the hope to reach out to me with your pitch as I walk by). Generally people who are interested will approach you, and do trust that they know in an instant whether it is the right fit for them. Sometimes they will make a quick first past and come back to you. Have a business card or postcard with your contact details and a visual reference available. I pick up a lot of cards at shows to remind me of designers to watch, and it is helpful if there is an immediate visual connection to the product. Style your booth and spend time on visual merchandising of your designs—include plants and fresh flowers and nice linen. Make it a beautiful, calm, visually pleasing space that makes buyers stop and feel welcome to enter the booth. Your booth design should complement and sell your product. Clearly display products and clearly indicate pricing and ordering terms. Do have a small, neat, clear product information/order form package ready to go. It should contain as much information as possible in as clear and concise a format as possible—your information, product images, wholesale pricing, recommended retail pricing, applicable order minimums, and terms. Offer me coffee, water, or a cold drink and a seat to rest my weary legs on if I am spending time in your booth . . . I also love small, quality gifts if I place an order! Walking the trade shows is tiring and it is nice to be treated when I enter a booth or place a significant order. Use your intuition, and be kind to the people you have a connection with. Make it easy for me to write an order! Have your order sheets ready, accept all methods of payment, and make it simple for me to give you my business details, tax ID information, and so on. Offer

low opening minimums. It encourages independent, small businesses to try new designers. Follow up with an email or, better still, a handwritten note of thanks after the fair. It sets you apart from the crowd. You can include a brief designer's bio, product images, and details that the buyer can use for promotional purposes once the buyer receives their order. Warmly greet past customers. On reorders, I always appreciate being able to switch out designs that have not sold well, to keep collections current and fresh. Walking away, you want buyers to leave your booth with the same enthusiasm for your product as you have."

—Jenah Barry, Owner, Xylem & Phloem

"Don't be too pushy; let the customer casually browse your booth and ask questions first. Do merchandise your booth well and have good lighting so your products shine, and have like products sit next to each other and are easy to find. Have postcards or line sheets to grab and go. They are super helpful when we review what we are following up on after a show. Have a tasteful sign that highlights anything special about your products that is attention grabbing and reiterates what you would normally say in a pitch."

—Erin Fergusson, Director of Merchandising, Rodale's

"Don't wrangle a buyer into your booth. It is simply rude. Also, when a buyer walks into a booth, the most often heard phrase is 'Are you familiar with this line?' Inevitably the person working the booth will venture into the long-winded spiel. If a buyer wants information, they will ask. It is way more inviting to start a conversation casually. It will disarm the buyer and make them feel more comfortable staying in the booth, not just feel like they are being sold and make them want to escape."

—Ashleigh Bergman, Senior Buyer for Jewelry, Anthropologie

"Be sure to circle back with contacts you met!"

—Julie Malone, Associate Buyer for Kitchen and Garden, Rodale's

"Some buyers like to be sold, coddled, wooed, pitched every line you have. I am the opposite. I prefer to be left alone to think. I know exactly what I like and what will work in my store, and I make quick decisions. Know what kind of buyer you have in front of you, and move forward accordingly."

—Silvana Costa, Buyer and Owner, The Wicked Peacock

"I think the biggest 'do' at a trade show is to be engaged. Be prepared to tell your story and be excited to share it with buyers whether it's 9 a.m. in the morning, or 6 p.m. after a long day! Passion, happiness, and good energy always shine through. Make your booth warm and welcoming. You don't always need to have your newest items up front—although a lot of designers do group their collections this way—I just think it's important that your booth is a reflection of your brand and the story you are telling for that season. And finally, I encourage designers to edit their collection and keep their displays clean and cohesive. It's such a cliché, but really true—less is more. I love a clean, crisp booth display. I know it's tempting to put everything out for buyers to see, but it can make a booth very cluttered. Be selective in what you choose to show. Show what you're proudest of and the top items that reflect who you are as a designer. You can always tuck away a few additional pieces to show if a buyer is really interested or send images of additional designs after the trade show."

—Sharon Hitchcock, Senior Buyer, UncommonGoods

"As a buyer, attending market can be really crazy. It is overstimulating and physically draining—but worth it. Everything starts to blend together after a while, so as a designer, you need to stand out! Don't expect the buyer to understand you or your brand based on your products alone. Make your booth an extension of your brand and vibe, whatever that means for you. Design your booth with the same artist's eye that you design your work, and display your logo and branding throughout the booth. A buyer should never have to ask what the name of your line is.

Also, have a chair for your buyer to sit. Offer water as a nice gesture as you're filling out paperwork (OK to reserve this just for your clients, not all browsers). I promise you it will be appreciated. And follow up right away, shortly after the show wraps. Recap my order, confirm the lead time, and add a personal touch to the experience. There are so many options to choose from that sometimes it comes down to simply who I enjoy working with on a personal level."

—Victoria Chiodo,
Retail Gallerist, Darioush

Any dos and don'ts for line sheets? What do you love and what do you not love?

"Line sheets should be comprehensive and clearly laid out. They should contain as much information as possible in as concise a format as possible—contact information, individual product images, wholesale pricing, recommended retail pricing, materials information, applicable order minimums, and terms. Color images are helpful. It works best to keep it neat and simple, but I also love an attractive package—fine paper or a lovely folder always leaves a great impression! In other words—attention to detail."

—Jenah Barry, Owner, Xylem & Phloem

"Definitely include pricing, materials, where/how the product is made—ALWAYS. Include great photographs of the products and clear style numbers so it is easy to communicate about the individual products. General information around inventory is always helpful—does the vendor carry stock, is product made to order with an x-week turnaround time."

—Erin Fergusson, Director
of Merchandising, Rodale's

"Short bio, good photography, material descriptions, prices. It doesn't interest me, but I know many buyers like to see press clippings and celeb shots as well. Keep it simple."

—Ashleigh Bergman, Senior Buyer
for Jewelry, Anthropologie

"Love straightforward catalogs with images, style number, and pricing. It's hard to cross-reference with complicated excel documents."

—Julie Malone, Associate Buyer for Kitchen and Garden, Rodale's

"Include PRICE, PICTURE, style number, color options, dimensions, materials."

—Silvana Costa, Buyer and Owner, The Wicked Peacock

"Line sheets should be as descriptive as possible—not only with item codes, but also with descriptions of what an item is, along with pricing. Aim for a clean, noncluttered sheet. And above all, make sure contact information is on the sheet. Buyers need to know who to call or email to place an order, or where to return samples after a review."

—Sharon Hitchcock, Senior Buyer, UncommonGoods

"Dos: Hire a good photographer if you can't photograph your work well yourself. Make sure style numbers, wholesale prices for each metal, and any other important info is included. Be as comprehensive as you can be.

Line sheets are a designer's first line of defense. It allows you to put your best foot forward when sending out emails, mailers, or a link to your website. If your line sheets look professional, boutiques and stores will treat you as a professional. If they look careless and sloppy, you will be immediately labeled an amateur and, more likely than not, your email will be sent to the trash."

—Camilla Gale, Buyer and Owner, Thistle & Clover

"Pictures are super helpful. When designing all of your collateral, think of it from the point of view of the buyer. At the end of the day, we're left with a stack of loose sheets, some with questionably legible writing. A good line sheet must have branding, should be easy to read and understand, and pictures are a major bonus. I suggest attempting to minimize the amount of hand writing while still maintaining an authentic, homespun feel."

—Victoria Chiodo, Retail Gallerist, Darioush

Where do you find most of the designers you work with?

"Large wholesale trade shows, small craft shows, studio visits, fine boutiques, galleries, museum stores, media and word of mouth, where inspiration strikes. Basically anywhere and everywhere, the trick is in joining all the dots and recognizing the difference between what you like and what will sell . . . and aiming to love what you sell. Also . . . while I don't particularly respond to cold-calling . . . if I am approached directly by a designer who is familiar with the products that I sell and is sincerely eager to work with me, who really seems excited by the work that I curate, I absolutely respond to that energy, if it is not pushy. Ask if you can set up an appointment with your favorite boutique. Flexibility, timing, and sincerity are key here—I often respond to a friendly designer who shows me their work and keeps the connection going. For bigger institutions, resonate with their mission and programming, and respect that they have specific processes and planning. But don't sit in your studio waiting to be discovered—make the connection and cultivate it where it is appropriate. As a buyer, it is personal connection that lifts you above the generic catalogs and solicitations. Why is your design a great fit for this particular retail avenue? Why is your product special? Why should the buyer care specifically about your product? Also, what are appealing terms for them? For example, consider a low opening minimum to get your work started."

—Jenah Barry, Owner, Xylem & Phloem

"Trade shows, blogs, Internet research, Instagram, competitive shopping, local craft fairs."

—Erin Fergusson, Director of Merchandising, Rodale's

"Trade shows, Internet research, traveling, and stopping people on the street to ask what they are wearing. Etsy, Pinterest, craft shows, and word of mouth as well."

—Ashleigh Bergman, Senior Buyer for Jewelry, Anthropologie

"Trade shows and blogs."

—Julie Malone, Associate Buyer for Kitchen and Garden, Rodale's

"Craft shows, trade shows, from online sourcing, Pinterest, etc. . . . I get creative!"

—Sharon Hitchcock, Senior Buyer, UncommonGoods

"Through our Open Call but also through word of mouth from other designers. You can be your peer's best champion!"

—Camilla Gale, Buyer and Owner, Thistle & Clover

"Blogs and digital magazines are a great source. Don't overlook the power of Instagram. I've made some great discoveries through tags and cross promotions on Instagram. It's amazing how many of the people I follow are all promoting each other. I believe this is the grassroots marketing of the future. People are really supporting each other. When you promote the people who inspire you, and they promote you in return, a community of your target demographic begins to take shape.

And don't discount trade shows, as there is nothing like meeting the designer face-to-face and touching the product."

—Victoria Chiodo,
Retail Gallerist, Darioush

What kind of information should a designer share about their company and designs?

"What inspires them—their visual inspiration, their design philosophy, important information on the makers of their designs (designer—maker/family business/made in the USA/fair trade . . .). What they love about making their work—why they enjoy their chosen medium, any special information about materials (conflict-free diamonds, recycled metals . . .). What they love about wearing the pieces that they create—the sensual, tactile, covetable,

wearable appeal of their jewelry. It's fine to keep it brief but have additional information handy. Easy-to-use care tips are useful. It's great to clarify your return and claims policy, and again, your flexibility will encourage future business. Giving the buyer everything that they need to sell the product makes it easy for them to do so and streamlines their inventory process."

—Jenah Barry, Owner, Xylem & Phloem

"Any philosophies about their business practices, what inspired them to start their company, what inspires their designs."

—Erin Fergusson, Director
of Merchandising, Rodale's

"Background before starting the line, where they draw inspiration, any industry-specific qualifications, special treatments, and methods/processes."

—Ashleigh Bergman, Senior Buyer
for Jewelry, Anthropologie

"Their company ethos and process is very important (Is it handmade? Is it recycled?) to communicate to the customer to establish price-value."

—Julie Malone, Associate Buyer
for Kitchen and Garden, Rodale's

"What inspires him/her."

—Silvana Costa, Buyer and Owner,
The Wicked Peacock

"A designer should not feel compelled to share sales data but should be able to speak about their capacity for production if asked, especially by a larger account. A designer should also be prepared to answer questions about materials, and in many cases, the origin of materials, as there is such a focus on ethically mined stones and metals. They should share as much about their technique as they are comfortable with—and the inspiration for a design or collection."

—Sharon Hitchcock, Senior Buyer,
UncommonGoods

"Store owners love to be able to share your story with their customers. Tell your story; tell what inspires you or your collection. The more context a customer has, the deeper connection they'll have to your designs."

—Camilla Gale, Buyer and Owner,
Thistle & Clover

"Just tell your story, the more authentic the better. I think now more than ever people want to know about the makers, the people behind the products. Talk about your inspiration, your history, your point of view, your process, whatever. Keep it light and positive, and focus on what makes you unique."

—Victoria Chiodo,
Retail Gallerist, Darioush

Anything else inspiring you'd like to add?

"It is important to me to love the things that I sell. I like to be able to tell clients a great story about the designers and products that I represent, so consider your packaging and artist's biography as elements of your work. There are so many things in the world . . . I like to believe that the pieces that I curate and sell are meaningful, beautiful, and special, that they have integrity, that they are designs to treasure, care about, and enjoy for a lifetime and pass on. My advice to designers is to create what they love and to make things that are truly special."

—Jenah Barry, Owner, Xylem & Phloem

"People love passion—let it show through in all you do! Consumers and buyers love connecting with passionate people; it really helps sell your product."

—Erin Fergusson, Director
of Merchandising, Rodale's

"From my experience on both sides of the coin (I used to design and co-own a jewelry line, too), I can tell you that most buyers love to meet the designers. So it is always nice if designers have a rep or showroom, that they accompany them to trade shows, trunk shows, or a few appointments. People want to know the designer's story, what inspires them, WHY they are doing what they are doing. They want to experience the designer's passion for what they do. It always bodes well for a designer to build a personal rapport with a client. When I was a designer, I always gave special clients pieces of the jewelry. It leaves a lasting impression, shows gratitude, and is also great publicity!"

—Ashleigh Bergman, Senior Buyer for Jewelry, Anthropologie

"One thing that I have noticed more than anything is that designers, especially new and emerging designers, need to BRAND their jewelry—as in actually create a label and solder it to the jewelry itself, or stamp the jewelry with a logo. (Alex and Ani is a GREAT example of well-branded jewelry.) Don't count on boutique owners to market your line for you, or to display any marketing materials you send along. Brand the work itself."

—Silvana Costa, Buyer and Owner, The Wicked Peacock

"The best designer/buyer relationships are true collaborations. While a buyer's job has a large component of data analysis and spreadsheets, I can say with absolute certainty that working with designers and seeing a collection become a reality is by far the best part of a buyer's job. It makes my heart happy to launch a designer's work into the world and see the excitement and reaction from our customers. I believe jewelry carries such emotion with it and that's why I love what I do."

—Sharon Hitchcock, Senior Buyer, UncommonGoods

"Make branding your best friend. More often than not, it's not the best designed products that sell, but the best branded. There is so much power in a strong brand identity. Consumers have more options and are more informed than ever before. If your brand identity is fully formed and super clear, consumers will form a connection with you. You're not just creating and selling jewelry, you're selling the idea of a lifestyle enhanced by the purchase."

—Victoria Chiodo, Retail Gallerist, Darioush

"Being successful in an arts/artisan/ crafts business is about more than just the mercantile—the exchange of money for goods. People like a story. The story helps people feel special about your work, feel good about purchasing it. Sometimes it can also make it fun, or make it sophisticated or elite—whatever it is that your story conveys. If you can create a story about your work, ultimately this makes a connection for people. These people you connect with become your clients, your students, your employees, your peers, your friends."

—Caroline Glemann, Owner and Designer, Liloveve Jewelry Studio

"Choose to believe that every 'no' you receive is simply a request for more information. Also, as my dad, the wisest man I know, told me, 'When you stop falling you stop learning.'"

—Melissa Joy Manning, Owner and Designer, Melissa Joy Manning

"Every basket we create requires care, thought, creativity, and attention to detail. The inspiration for our baskets comes from our clients who value our business, our flexibility, and versatility. We tell people that the sky's the limit on what we can develop. Our clients, in turn, challenge us to develop baskets that are unique and different. We get

our energy, drive, and inspiration from those around us. We could not ask for a greater level of inspiration."

—Elena Yearly, Owner, Nostalgia Baskets

"Building a sustainable jewelry business (or any business, for that matter) is very difficult. Be persistent, be innovative, and stay true to yourself!"

—Sarah Greenberg, Owner and Designer, Sarah Swell

Where should someone start if they want to learn how to make jewelry? What classes should they take?

"Foundation classes can be a great place to start. Basic wax carving. Basic silver/ metalsmithing. Alloying with gold— tapping into a most ancient way of working with metal—milling and forging. Getting the 'feeling' for the metal in your hands, so you can develop the meditative, sensitive place that 'understands' the material and allow the designs to spring from this knowledge. Alternatively, many people wish to start with a design that they like and attempt to bring the material into the desired shape, instead of starting with a more exploratory approach and working with the properties of the materials. Both ways will work; the second just requires more repetition and practice to achieve good technique and consistent results."

—Caroline Glemann, Owner and Designer, Liloveve Jewelry Studio

What is the most challenging part of working with clients on custom pieces?

"One of the most challenging parts of custom design is cultivating the trust that is necessary between artist and client. You often start by talking about ideas with another person, who may or may not share the same descriptive language that you have. You have to be perceptive to what elements of design are most important to your client. In addition, you have to assess the costs of materials and time, assess your client's budget, as well as problem solve in making something that you may have never made exactly before.

The artist has to trust the client that they are conveying as accurately as they can their ideas and budget, while trusting oneself to create it, and the client needs to trust the artist that some elements of design may shift slightly during the design process and that the artist is working to the best of their ability to make the piece perfect. Because custom design is a challenging process, it can also be very rewarding work."

—Caroline Glemann, Owner and Designer, Liloveve Jewelry Studio

Where do you find your retail clients and/or retail outlets?
"Word of mouth. Internet."

—Caroline Glemann, Owner and Designer, Liloveve Jewelry Studio

"Many of my direct retail sales come from my storefront, which includes our studio and showroom space. Customers learn about my work by finding me on social media or from local press. I do sell online as well, but feel that the connection between an item of jewelry and the customer happens when they can try it on in person. Finding a way to be accessible to your customers in real life and not just virtually is very important and creates repeat clients, which are the best kind!"

—Sarah Greenberg, Owner and Designer, Sarah Swell

"I find that wearing my designs have brought me many retail clients and my best retail outlets. People always say the designer wears their designs best, and

I have found that to be very helpful in gaining new customers. My collection is all about mixing, matching, and stacking, and I wear A LOT at a time! When people see how the jewelry should be worn, they usually buy right off of me."

—Lacey Seltzer, Owner and Designer, Lacey Ryan Jewelry

What has been the most difficult decision you've had to make while running a business?

"Time management. Time management. Time management."

—Caroline Glemann, Owner and Designer, Liloveve Jewelry Studio

"How to balance personal and professional obligations."

—Melissa Joy Manning, Owner and Designer, Melissa Joy Manning

"I'd say the decision to become completely self-employed. There was a time when I was simultaneously running my business and working full time for another designer. After I left that job to focus on my own business, I continued to pursue part-time work as a safety net. Finally taking the leap to being supported entirely by my business was a scary one,

but it wasn't until that moment that I was really 'all in.'"

—Sarah Greenberg, Owner and Designer, Sarah Swell

How do you find your resources (materials, stone setters, casters, etc.)?

"I trust my instincts. People who love what they do will put in effort and strive for a good result—this is just natural. I look for these people. I do not put too much faith in paper statements (conflict-free, green, ethically sourced, etc) even though they do offer some reassurance. I look at the quality of the materials, the attention to detail of the person, their inherent curiosity about how things work. I believe that people who love what they do will always make time when possible to answer your questions and seek answers if they do not have them."

—Caroline Glemann, Owner and Designer, Liloveve Jewelry Studio

"The best way to find nearly any kind of resource is by being connected with other jewelers. I'm very lucky to be surrounded by a community of designers that are willing to share information. It is truly invaluable to create relationships with others in your field, especially one that is so difficult to navigate, like the jewelry industry. Be kind, honest, and open, and generally others will be, too!

—Sarah Greenberg, Owner
and Designer, Sarah Swell

"Because I have been making jewelry for many years, I have met a TON of people along the way. I have been working with some of my vendors now for over ten years. Going to Tucson and meeting new vendors was great for me. It's so important to speak to anyone and everyone you meet who is in the jewelry industry. I have found great casters and have been set up with great manufacturers in NYC just by speaking with someone in a coffee shop or a friend of a friend. It's been extremely helpful!"

—Lacey Seltzer, Owner
and Designer, Lacey Ryan Jewelry

How did you get started making jewelry?

"I started making jewelry as a hobby when I was just nine years old. I would make jewelry and sell it on my red wagon in Fire Island. Once I realized I could make money doing something I loved, I knew it was something I would do forever."

—Lacey Seltzer, Owner
and Designer, Lacey Ryan Jewelry

"I made my first necklace when I was four—I've never stopped making jewelry since."

—Melissa Joy Manning, Owner
and Designer, Melissa Joy Manning

"While in art school, I was working for a jeweler in retail sales. During this time, I became infatuated with jewelry and took a metalsmithing class just for fun. I knew that I wanted to pursue being a designer and promptly dropped out of art school. I decided to attend a more jewelry-specific trade school (Revere Academy of Jewelry Arts) to acquire technical skills. Afterward, I worked for several different designers and jewelers with the goal of learning as much about the industry as I could. I launched my business in 2008 and have never looked back!

—Sarah Greenberg, Owner
and Designer, Sarah Swell

Where do you find your inspiration?

"I'm inspired by all that surrounds me. I can be in the most random place and find inspiration there. I also love to travel and have been lucky enough to travel to many countries around the world. It's extremely inspiring being out of your element and seeing art and culture from other places."

—LACEY SELTZER, OWNER
AND DESIGNER, LACEY RYAN JEWELRY

"Travel, people, and stones."

—MELISSA JOY MANNING, OWNER
AND DESIGNER, MELISSA JOY MANNING

"Many different places! Much of my work is nature inspired; however, I also draw heavily from ancient jewelry. In addition, I look at current trends in jewelry, fashion, and interiors and take them into account to some degree."

—SARAH GREENBERG, OWNER
AND DESIGNER, SARAH SWELL

What is your design process like? How many collections do you come out with in a year, and how do you stick to your schedule?

"I'm always designing in some sense. Most days, I'm at least thinking about new jewelry, and several days a week I break out my sketchbook. I allow myself to do this freely without thinking too hard about the ideas that come forward. This way, when I'm ready to turn drawings into reality, I have tons of material to work with. If I just sit down without first hashing out design ideas and have to create a collection, it feels

very forced to me. I need more time for it all to settle. I introduce two small collections a year to coincide with the trade shows I do. Essentially a fall/winter and spring/summer line; however, I don't stick to as strict of a schedule as the fashion calendar."

—SARAH GREENBERG, OWNER
AND DESIGNER, SARAH SWELL

"I usually come out with two definite collections each year (spring and fall) and then add in some special items for holiday and summer. I work with a sales rep, who usually gives me a time frame for when she needs the new collections, and I work around her appointments and schedules. I have some moments where I have trouble thinking of newness, but once I do some trend research and shop the markets, my head is filled with new ideas!"

—LACEY SELTZER, OWNER
AND DESIGNER, LACEY RYAN JEWELRY

"I design constantly. We have over two thousand active SKUs and are constantly merchandising the collection through additions and subtractions to the collection. My design schedule is made at the start of every year and keeping to it is key—if I'm late, we can't go to market."

—MELISSA JOY MANNING, OWNER
AND DESIGNER, MELISSA JOY MANNING

Any tips for wholesale trade shows? How did you decide when to start showing at trade shows and which one?

"I've only participated in one trade show—Capsule a few years ago. I have decided to not take the trade-show approach because I am very happy with my sales rep. I always consider doing one, but I usually get nervous! I've heard many different opinions on whether or not they are worth it. I do believe it's great exposure for your brand, especially if you are not part of a showroom. Displays are key!"

—Lacey Seltzer, Owner
and Designer, Lacey Ryan Jewelry

"Wholesale trade shows are marketing investments first and foremost. Looking at your trade-show goals long term and understanding them to be brand-building exercises are key to building a competitive company in the marketplace."

—Melissa Joy Manning, Owner
and Designer, Melissa Joy Manning

"Wholesale is a great route to pursue if you want to build a solid base for your business. Trade shows really are the quickest way to acquire new accounts. Many of the shows are expensive and complicated, so definitely do your

research before selecting which one is right for you. If possible, visit a few to get a sense of the amount of traffic and general mood of the exhibitors. Make sure you pick a show that has designers that fall within your price point and is attended by buyers that you hope to make connections with. Also, be patient! It takes time to build relationships and buyers often want to see you for a few seasons before they invest in you."

—Sarah Greenberg, Owner
and Designer, Sarah Swell

How have you chosen sales reps and/or showrooms before? Any advice on making the right choice?

"I actually found my current sales rep through Instagram! I came across her page and it ended up that we had a mutual friend in common. I got very lucky; it's been a huge success!"

—Lacey Seltzer, Owner
and Designer, Lacey Ryan Jewelry

"You are the best representation for your brand—only you can tell your authentic story. Partnering with a sales rep or agency is an important choice—never choose quickly and always choose someone who has solid contacts, a good reputation, and is passionate about your brand. Never work with someone who speaks badly about anybody."

—Melissa Joy Manning, Owner and Designer, Melissa Joy Manning

Have you ever had a bad experience with a sales rep? Good experience?
"Finding a good sales rep/showroom is so hard! You really want to be completely comfortable and confident that your sales rep gets your line. I have worked with people in the past who have 'liked' my collection, but it turned out they didn't have the right customer to buy it. I have been promised a lot by salespeople and have been very disappointed. My current situation is so successful because my sales rep wears my collection, she is my target customer and has the relationship with the right buyers for my brand."

—Lacey Seltzer, Owner and Designer, Lacey Ryan Jewelry

How have you dealt with scaling up your production? (Hiring in-house bench jewelers, outsourcing to independent contractors, factory, etc.)
"This has been a difficult one for me. Having started my business on a shoestring budget, I've always been wary of adding extra expenses to my business. For a long time I tried to do everything myself to cut

costs and maintain control by keeping all aspects of my business in-house. This results only in exhaustion! I'd suggest asking for help as soon as you become overwhelmed, in whatever capacity you can afford. If you take time to manage work flow from the beginning, you'll be prepared to handle growth when it comes. Currently we have two bench jewelers on staff that work from our studio. We outsource our casting and some stone setting, but everything else we do in-house."

—Sarah Greenberg, Owner and Designer, Sarah Swell

Where do you find your clients that you represent, or how do they find you?
"Over the last four years, I've curated a list of about three thousand brands that fit the COEUR aesthetic. Some of the brands had been on my radar for some time and others were new discoveries that simply fell into my lap. Before launching COEUR, I ran a very connected sales and press showroom, eM Productions, for about ten years, where we worked closely with an array of accessories and ready-to-wear brands. Some of them were new and others were established, and having knowledge of stores and buyer connections helped me create a strong list of lines. I

also travel quite a bit visiting stores all over to see who they are buying and what's new on the market. These days, we have many buyers who are fond of COEUR recommend some of their favorite lines to us to show during market. Brands that have done very well at the show always speak highly of it and spread the word to brands they feel would be a good fit."

—Henri Meyers, Cofounder and Creative Director, COEUR trade show

How does a designer find a sales rep or showroom, and how do you know if it is a good fit?

"These days, it's tricky to lock in and find the right showroom or sales agent for any brand. It really depends on the showroom and the other brands they sell and if there is room to fit in another line. The best way is to arrange a meeting with the sales agent or showroom to discuss their outreach and how they can work for you to grow the line."

—Henri Meyers, Cofounder and Creative Director, COEUR trade show

Any tips for wholesale trade shows? How does a brand decide what show to exhibit at?

"There are lots of great shows but not all are right. The best is to walk the shows to see which brands are participating and, if you have the time, chat up a line to gauge their experience. Mind you, not everyone will have the same experience. Brands that make appointments prior to the show always have a better run than those who are just starting out. Trade shows take time, and one must commit to at least three seasons to really gauge how things go. General atmosphere and vibe also play a part in choosing the right show for you."

—Henri Meyers, Cofounder and Creative Director, COEUR trade show

Any trade show don'ts you've seen?

"Trade show don'ts . . . well, there is always some dead time, and although some brands get worried and feel the show is 'slow,' that's the perfect time to research stores, get on your social media outlets—Twitter, Facebook, and Instagram—to try and connect with those stores that could be a fit/match for your brand. Many brands keep their heads locked on their phones or laptops and this is a major no-no . . . you want to be engaging and pleasant when buyers are around. The worst thing I see is when a buyer comes near a booth and the salesperson or designer is not paying attention or looks grumpy or maybe just not even at their booth, they miss out on a potential sale. No one wants to approach someone who looks disinterested or unhappy. Turn that frown upside down and get active. Be present and smile. Know the product and vibe the buyers. Don't attack them if they show interest; just take a breath and engage them slowly. If they like the line, they will inquire. Get a business card and reconnect with them postshow."

—Henri Meyers, Cofounder and Creative Director, COEUR trade show

What do you think the best way for brands to reach out to potential stores is besides a trade show?

"Prior to market week is ALWAYS suggested—trying to contact a buyer during market week is never good unless you already have a relationship with them. Buyers are very busy and during show season are rarely at the stores. Again, being on social media could also help grab the attention of those buyers. Just last season, we had not one or two but four buyers come to the show after seeing posts and images from brands showing at COEUR. Brands can also try to make appointments with the buyers in store, but ultimately, having a good, strong image and product that is sellable will warrant the attention of those buyers to meet with you and write your brand."

—Henri Meyers, Cofounder and Creative Director, COEUR trade show

How do you define 'fair trade'?

"'Fair trade' to me means 'buying fair' across the board—whether we are talking about jewelry, woven baskets, finely crafted goods, farmed goods. According to a *Giftware News* article in their December 2014 publication, 'Fair trade is a vibrant movement that continues to grow as consumers look to find out where their dollars are going. With promises of fair wages, economic development, and sustainability at the heart of the fair trade community, it is no surprise that retailers are actively taking stock in these products.' This is how I view fair trade and I could not have said it better."

—Elena Yearly, Owner, Nostalgia Baskets

How do you find fair trade vendors?

"Fortunately, there are numerous sources for locating fair trade vendors. They can be found through local area boutiques, at international gifting conferences and their Maker's Market exhibitors, and through my relationship with Handmade in America. Industry publications such as *Giftware News*, *Smart Retailer*, and *Museums & More* and others frequently publish articles on fair trade and call special attention to fair trade vendors in the US and abroad. I pay attention to those organizations whose mission is fair trade (i.e., the Fair Trade Federation, Fair Trade USA, World Fair Trade Organization, and others) and to their members as resources to locate vendors who we would like to buy from to include in our gift baskets."

—Elena Yearly, Owner,
Nostalgia Baskets

How did you know which type of business to form and what was right for you?

"Business opportunities can emerge when you least expect. I was entrenched in my finance corporate career. Yet, something was missing, and I knew I really wanted to tap into and demonstrate my creative and entrepreneurial sides. Therefore, I thought back to my childhood and the gift basket creations I would hand make for family members. In 2001, I helped my mom celebrate a landmark occasion (the anniversary of her immigration to the US) by creating a basket that was totally customized and personalized around her, her life, and interests. Her emotional reaction was priceless. I started attending gifting trade shows and conferences whenever I had a free moment. We then started to create unique 'celebration of life'

gift baskets with no two being the same and centered around people's personal histories and lives. This is when I knew what business I wanted to form. It was exactly what I was looking for from a creative and entrepreneurial standpoint. Nostalgia Baskets was born as a part-time business with my studio in my home. Now, over fourteen years, we have developed a real niche for ourselves in the customization gift basket arena. We have been selling our unique brand and line of one-of-a-kind gift baskets worldwide for well over a decade. People (complete strangers) get just as emotional as my mom. Now we help people feel special around the globe through our gift basket creations that 'tug at the heart.'"

—Elena Yearly, Owner,
Nostalgia Baskets

How has your education played a part in your business?

"Education has played a major role in the formation and development of Nostalgia Baskets. I feel that my formal education, with a masters in business administration from Colorado State, along with a number of business-related certifications, has helped to propel and enhance what we bring to the table as a gifting company.

There is also the informal education—learning from other online retailers, learning from artisans, observing handmade and gifting trends—that has allowed me to reach a stage in my gifting career whereby now I am tapped as a handmade and custom gifting expert to speak at industry conferences."

—Elena Yearly, Owner,
Nostalgia Baskets

What lessons have you learned about being an entrepreneur?

"The lessons keep coming. I have learned that I have to constantly keep current yet stay focused on where my business is headed and where I would like it to be over time. I have had to learn to stay away from being distracted. Those distractions are all around us—from people, social media, the idea of the moment. I have learned to balance all the positive feedback we get with making strategic and informed decisions that make sense for the company. Further, I have learned to make important and quick adjustments to my business model as needed to ensure the business continues to move forward properly."

—Elena Yearly, Owner,
Nostalgia Baskets

What mistakes have you made?

"Over time, people have given us such great feedback on the baskets we have created and sent both domestically and overseas. In retrospect, I wish I had captured their feedback in writing. That is the mistake I made—not to have requested written reviews from the outset. We are having to play catch-up with testimonials now."

—Elena Yearly, Owner,
Nostalgia Baskets

Glossary

✦

2%Net10: A payment term between buyer and vendor. Payment is sent to the vendor within ten days after products received with a 2 percent discount.

925: The short name for sterling silver; 92.5% fine silver and, typically, 7.5% copper.

Alloy: A mixture of two or more metallic elements, combined to give greater strength or alter color.

Base price: The cost of materials and labor, in dollars, that goes into every piece you sell; this covers the cost of your prototype.

Carat: A unit of measure for precious gemstones and pearls; equivalent to 200 milligrams.

COGS (cost of goods sold): Cost of production for goods, including materials and labor.

Consignment: Offering products for sale at a physical store, with the maker paid when an item sells.

Cost: The dollar amount that it costs you to make each jewelry piece, including the base price, materials, and labor.

DBA (doing business as): A designation indicating that your business is being conducted under a different name than the legal business name.

DWT: Abbreviation for pennyweight, sometimes seen as PWT. A unit of measure used to weigh metal—24 grains, or $\frac{1}{20}$ of a troy ounce.

EIN (employer identification number): A number you are required to get, if you operate as a corporation or a partnership, to put on tax documents.

FOB destination (free on board): A term used to specify that the seller transfers ownership of goods to the buyer once they reach the final delivery point. Therefore the seller is responsible for the goods while they are being delivered.

FOB shipping point (free on board): A term used to specify that the seller transfers ownership of goods to the buyer once they leave the seller and are out for delivery. Therefore the buyer is responsible for the goods while they are being delivered.

Gram: A unit of measure; $\frac{1}{1000}$ of a kilogram.

Gross profit: Sales revenue minus cost of goods sold.

Gross: Twelve dozen, or 144.

Karat: A measure of the purity of gold; pure gold is 24 karats.

LOR (letter of responsibility): Used for press pulls. The stylist or the publication borrowing the items gives an LOR to the vendor declaring responsibility for all items borrowed if any are damaged or lost while in their care.

MAP (minimum advertised price): A price established by the manufacturer and agreed upon by the reseller. This policy is in place to make sure a reseller doesn't undersell the product, especially when selling online.

Metal: A pure element found in the earth.

Model: The prototype created for a production line.

Mold: A two-part form used to duplicate models. Silicone and rubber molds are most commonly used in the jewelry industry.

MSRP (manufacturer's suggested retail price): A retail price suggested by the manufacturer.

Net profit: Total earnings after subtracting all expenses.

Net30: A payment term between buyer and vendor. Payment is sent to the vendor thirty days after products are received.

PO (purchase order): A document from the buyer to the seller specifying what products and quantities the buyer would like to buy.

Retail markup: Most retailers mark up wholesale between 200% and 250%, depending on their customers. Average markup is 220%, so generate your retail price by multiplying your wholesale by 2.2.

Retail: Selling goods directly to the public.

Sales margin: The difference between revenue and cost. Subtract the COGS from the price of an item.

SKU (stock keeping unit): An alphanumeric code created by the maker for inventory and ordering purposes.

Spec sheet (speculation sheet): A technical document with measurement and material information on how a product is made.

Sprue: A channel through which molten metal is poured during the lost-wax casting process.

TIN (taxpayer identification number): A general term for a number a business or individual uses on tax documents for the IRS.

TOP sample (top of production sample): An exact representation of a product in color, shape, and size, usually sent to a buyer for approval and to compare for quality control.

Troy ounce: A unit of measure used to weigh metal; 480 grains and 20 pennyweights.

UPC (universal product code): A universal bar code system used to keep track of products in a warehouse.

Wholesale: The discounted price of a product available to resellers when purchased in bulk.

Work harden: The process of making metal tough by hammering or otherwise manipulating it.

Resource List

✦

Even if you're not producing or selling locally, many of these vendors produce and ship for designers worldwide.

Contractors

AJC
www.ajcjewelryny.com
247 West 30th Street, #302
New York, NY 10001
212-594-3703
All jewelry finishing. Model making, mold making, casting, finishing, stone setting, and polishing.

The Laser Booth
www.thelaserbooth.com
44 West 47th Street, Suite 3
New York, NY 10036
212-382-2299
CAD design, model making, fabrication, stone setting, laser cutting, and laser welding.

Gemstone and Bead Suppliers

Columbia Gem House, Inc.
www.columbiagemhouse.com
PO Box 820889
Vancouver, WA 98682
360-514-0569
Specializing in fair trade gemstones.

Fire Mountain Gems
www.firemountaingems.com
1 Fire Mountain Way
Grants Pass, OR 97526

1-800-423-2319
Offering beads and tools; online and by mail order.

Rough Diamond World
www.roughdiamondworld.com
71 West 47th Street, #1001
New York, NY 10036
212-758-0130
Specializing in rough and unusual diamonds.

Jewelry Trade Schools and University Programs—United States

Noteworthy University Programs

California College of the Arts
www.cca.edu
5212 Broadway
Oakland, CA 94618
510-594-3600

Cranbrook Academy of Art
www.cranbrookart.edu
39221 Woodward Avenue
Bloomfield Hills, MI 48303
248-645-3300

Fashion Institute of Technology
www.fitnyc.edu
227 West 27th Street
New York, NY 10001
212-217-7999

Indiana University Bloomington
www.indiana.edu
107 S. Indiana Avenue
Bloomington, IN 47405
812-855-4848

Rhode Island School of Design
www.risd.edu
2 College Street
Providence, RI 02903
401-454-6100

Savannah College of Art and Design
www.scad.edu
342 Bull Street
Savannah, GA 31402
912-525-5100

SUNY New Paltz
www.newpaltz.edu
1 Hawk Drive
New Paltz, NY 12561
845-257-7869

Syracuse University
vpa.syr.edu
202 Crouse College
Syracuse, NY 13244
315-443-2769

Temple University
www.temple.edu
1801 N. Broad Street
Philadelphia, PA 19122
215-204-7000

University of Wisconsin-Madison
www.wisc.edu
702 W. Johnson Street, Suite 1101
Madison, WI 53715
608-262-3961

Virginia Commonwealth University
www.vcu.edu
821 W. Franklin Street
Richmond, VA 23284
804-828-0100

Noteworthy Trade Schools and Studios

92nd Street Y Jewelry Center
www.92y.org/SOA/Jewelry.aspx
1395 Lexington Avenue
New York, NY 10128
212-415-5564

American Jewelers Institute
www.jewelersschool.org
PO Box 225
Columbia City, OR 97018
1-800-309-7540

Arrowmont School of Arts and Crafts
www.arrowmont.org
556 Parkway
Gatlinburg, TN 37738
865-436-5860

Brookfield Craft Center
www.brookfieldcraft.org
286 Whisconier Road
Brookfield, CT. 06804
203-775-4526

Brooklyn Metal Works
bkmetalworks.com
640 Dean Street
Brooklyn, NY 11238
347-762-4757

California Institute of Jewelry Training
www.jewelrytraining.com
5805 Windmill Way
Carmichael, CA 95608
916-487-1122

Colorado Academy of Silversmithing
silversmithing.homestead.com/SilverClasses1.
html
PO Box 2433
Estes Park, CO 80517
303-517-1068

Conner Jewelers School
151 East Main Street
New Albany, IN 47150
812-944-1798
jewelersschool.net

Gemological Institute of America
www.gia.edu
5345 Armada Drive
Carlsbad, CA 92008
976-603-4000

Haystack Mountain School of Crafts
www.haystack-mtn.org
PO Box 518
Deer Isle, ME 04627
207-348-2306

Howard Academy for the Metal Arts
516 East Main Street
Stoughton, WI 53589
608-873-5199
www.howard-academy.com

Jewelry Arts Institute
www.jewelryarts.com
22 East 49th Street, 4th Floor
New York, NY 10017
212-362-8633

Liloveve Jewelry Studio
www.liloveve.com
457 Grand Street
Brooklyn, NY 11211
718-388-2190

Metalwerx
www.metalwerx.com
50 Guinan Street
Waltham, MA 02451
781-937-3532

New Approach School for Jewelers
www.newapproachschool.com
107 SE Parkway Court
Franklin, TN 37064
1-800-529-4763

North Bennet Street School
http://www.nbss.edu
150 North Street
Boston, MA 02109
617-227-0155

Penland School of Craft
www.penland.org
67 Doras Trail
Penland, NC 28765
828-765-2359

Revere Academy of Jewelry Arts
www.revereacademy.com
785 Market Street, Suite 900
San Francisco, CA 94103
415-391-4179

Southwest School of Art
www.swschool.org
300 Augusta Street
San Antonio, TX 78205
210-224-1848

Stewart's International School For Jewelers
www.stewartsintlschool.com
651 W. Indiantown Road
Jupiter, FL 33458
1-800-843-3409

Studio Jewelers
www.studiojewelersltd.com
32 East 31st Street, #3
New York, NY 10016
212-686-1944

Texas Institute of Jewelry Technology at Paris Junior College
www.parisjc.edu/index.php/tijt
2400 Clarksville Street
Paris, TX 75460
1-800-232-5804

Touchstone Center For Crafts
http://www.touchstonecrafts.org
1049 Wharton Furnace Road
Farmington, PA 15437
1-800-721-0177
Short classes in metalsmithing, setting, casting and inlay work.

Lapidary
R Gems
www.gemstonecutters.com
48 West 48th Street, 2nd Floor
New York, NY 10036
212-302-3388
Cutting and polishing semiprecious and precious gemstones. Wide selection of natural and synthetic gemstones.

Metal and Tool Suppliers
All Craft Jewelry Supply
135 West 29th Street, #205
New York, NY 10001
212-279-7077
Tools and equipment; in person and by mail order.

Gesswein
www.gesswein.com
201 Hancock Avenue, P.O. Box 3998
Bridgeport, CT 06605
1-800-243-4466
Tools and equipment; in person, by mail order, and online.

Hoover and Strong
www.hooverandstrong.com
10700 Trade Road
N. Chesterfield, VA 23236
1-800-759-9997
Precious metals and tools. Specializing in recycled metals.

Metalliferous
www.metalliferous.com
34 West 46th Street, 3rd Floor
New York, NY 10036
212-944-0909
Silver and base metals, findings, chain, tools, and new and used equipment; online, in person, and by mail order.

Myron Tobak
www.myrontobak.com
25 West 47th Street
New York, NY 10036
212-398-8300
Precious metal sheet, wire, and findings, and some tools.

Otto Frei
www.ottofrei.com
126 2nd Street
Oakland, CA 94607
1-800-772-3456
Metal, tools, and equipment; in person, by mail order, and online.

Rio Grande
www.riogrande.com
7500 Bluewater Rd NW
Albuquerque, NM 87121
800-545-6566
Gemstones, metal, and findings; tools and equipment; display and packaging materials via mail order catalog and online.

Ross Metals
www.rossmetals.com
27 West 47th Street
New York, NY 10036
800-654-7677
Precious metal sheet, wire, and findings; in person, by mail order, and online. Requires tax ID.

Zak Tools
www.zakjewelrytools.com
55 West 47th Street, 2nd Floor
New York, NY 10036
212-768-8122
Tools and equipment; in person, by mail order, and online.

Metal Casters

Carrera Casting
www.carreracasting.com
64 West 48th Street, 2nd Floor
New York, NY 10036
212-869-8762
CAD designers, mold makers, and metal casting of precious metals.

Roni Casting
33 West 46th Street, 7th Floor
New York, NY 10036
212-869-1432
Mold makers, metal casting of base and precious metals, and stainless-steel casting.

Taba Casting
www.tabacast.com
2 West 46th Street, #315
New York, NY 10036
212-354-6792
CAD designers, mold makers, and metal casting of precious and base metals.

Metal Platers

Daniel Simon Plating
64 West 48th Street, #1307
New York, NY 10036
212-819-0889
Metal plating.

Red Sky Plating
www.redskyplating.com
630 Oak Street SE
Albuquerque, NM 87106
505-243-6600
Metal plating and finishing.

T and M Plating
www.tandmplating.com
357 West 36th Street
New York, NY 10036
212-967-1110
Metal plating.

Packaging

Packaging Specialities
www.pack-spec.com
3 Opportunity Way
Newburyport, MA 01950
800-722-7732
Standard and custom packaging.

Uline
www.uline.com
12575 Uline Drive
Pleasant Prairie, WI 53158
800-295-5510
Packaging, shipping, and office supplies; online, by mail order, and at one of their eleven locations throughout North America.

Photo Editing

Clipping Magic
www.clippingmagic.com
Photo editing and background removal service.

Printing Companies

Overnight Prints
www.overnightprints.com
888-677-2000
Inexpensive printing service, templates, and custom work.

Vista Print
www.vistaprint.com
866-614-8002
Inexpensive printing service, templates, and custom work.

Stamps

Sossner Steel Stamps
www.sossnerstamps.com
180 Don Lewis Boulevard
Elizabethtown, TN 37643
800-828-9515
Standard and custom-made metal stamps.

Sparks Steel Stamps
37-26 34th Street
Long Island City, NY 11101
718-729-7506
Standard and custom-made metal stamps.

Website Template Companies

Domain.com
www.domain.com
Domain and web hosting.

Squarespace
www.squarespace.com
Domain and web hosting, website templates, and e-commerce.

Wix
www.wix.com
Domain and web hosting, website templates, and e-commerce.

Acknowledgments

✦

Writing this book has been a true honor and a collaborative effort. I'd like to thank my mom for encouraging me to do what I love and follow the path not always taken. This book is dedicated to you. I'd like to thank my dad for instilling the entrepreneurial spirit in me. And most of all I'd like to thank my husband, Ben, for being my support system, whether lugging furniture to a trade show, talking through ideas, or editing this book. You are the eye of my storm.

I'd like to acknowledge the incredible support from my friends and family. There are too many to name, but you know who you are.

I'm so grateful to the wonderful buyers, designers, and industry experts who shared their input for this book— Jenah Barry, Erin Fergusson, Ashleigh Bergman, Julie Malone, Silvana Costa, Sharon Hitchcock, Camilla Gale, Victoria Chiodo, Caroline Glemann, Melissa Joy Manning, Elena Yearly, Lacey Seltzer, Sarah Greenberg, Henri Meyers, Rand Niederhoffer, the Taba Casting team, and all the folks at Etsy.

I'm grateful beyond words to my editor, Diana Ventimiglia. Thank you for presenting this project to me, for challenging me to put my lessons on paper, and for your patience. Thank you to the whole team at Sterling Publishing.

Thank you to all my wonderful teachers of all kinds—professors, employers, employees, and friends. My professors at Syracuse University, Barbara Walter and Lori Hawk, who gave me an incredible foundation and sparked a curiosity for materials inside me. Caroline Glemann of Liloveve Jewelry Studio, thank you for teaching me how to teach.

And lastly, thank you to all my students—past and future. Your creativity and eagerness to learn are so inspiring. That keeps me learning every single day.

About the Author

✦

Emilie Shapiro currently lives and works in New York City. She is the head designer of her jewelry line, Emilie Shapiro Contemporary Metals. Emilie's work is inspired by natural elements and heavily driven by experimentation and process, and incorporates rough gemstones, celebrating beauty in imperfection. Emilie's work is sold worldwide at locations such as the American Natural History Museum, Anthropologie, and UncommonGoods. Emilie frequently teaches workshops on jewelry production and wax carving at the 92nd Street Y, Liloveve Jewelry Studio, and the Brooklyn Museum of Art, as well as at other studios throughout the New York metropolitan area. She received her BFA in jewelry and metalsmithing from Crouse College, Syracuse University, and studied at Alchimia, a contemporary jewelry school in Florence, Italy.

Photography Credits

✦

Index

✦